Life on This Catskills Farm

Life on This
Catskills Farm

EDWARD LAMB NICHOLS, JR.

ISBN 979-8-8545716-5-4

Front cover photo by Ray Brizzi

"Half Walking," "Banking the House," and "The Smell of Electricity" originally appeared, in slightly different form, in *Catskill Tri-County Historical Views*.

Production of this volume was made possible by a generous grant from the A. Lindsay & Olive B. O'Connor Foundation

In Appreciation

Early on a phrase that I heard quite often was "Write it down." So now I have. My daughter Norma, who has been right up to her ears in family history and genealogy for years, was the lead cheerleader in this effort. Without her dedicated encouragement I may never have had the pleasure of recalling so many of my past experiences. Sometimes dealing with one memory leads to remembering something else that I had completely forgotten about. Thanks, Norma.

Going back and reading my mother's diaries has jogged my memory. For writing things down, thanks so much, Mom.

Remembering the stories my father told, some that he lived, fills in additional information and sometimes, entire story lines for me. Thanks, Dad.

To my wife Bea for helping me to get started, then acting as my personal editor. For finding out about a local writers group associated with the Stamford Library, then encouraging me to join them. That writers group and a later-formed one associated with the Delhi Library have provided much encouragement. Thanks Bea.

To my niece, Gwen, and to her husband, Paul, for helping me along the way in more ways than one. Gwen and Paul own the house that I was born in and grew up in. I now, after a sixty-eight-year hiatus, live in an apartment in that house. They keep track of me and come in with ideas and information to help me. Thank you both for all your caring.

Finally, to Terry Bradshaw, another member of the Stamford Library Writers Circle, who has been instrumental in taking my stories from sheets of paper to an actual book. After hearing one of my stories she suggested it and two others for publication in *Catskill Tri-County Historical Views*. Seeing them in print encouraged me even further. Many thanks to Terry.

I wish to extend my sincere appreciation to all those mentioned or unmentioned who have helped along the way.

Ed Nichols

Contents

Edward Lamb Nichols, Sr., circa 1935

NOTE: The stories in this book took place on and around our family farm. So that this first story title doesn't deceive the reader, this is not a sheep farm, although sheep have been kept on it at least twice during its history. It is named for its original settler.

The Lamb Farm

The picture opposite is of my father, Ed Nichols, Sr., holding a lamb in his arms. This picture was taken in the mid-1930s behind the house that he and his family lived in, a house built by his ancestors, the Lambs. This was their backyard and the chimney of the original fireplace built into the house is in view. The fireplace is still intact today but is not used. The framing of the house indicates there could have been a fireplace on the other gable end also.

The Lamb family lived in a log cabin built by Patrick Lamb when he first settled the homestead. Living in the log cabin allowed them to construct a fairly modern home for the times and do it over several years. It was not completed all in one year as all the lumber and timbers were cut on the farm and skidded to the work site by oxen. The logs were either sawed or chopped by hand to make the supplies they needed. Sawmills were sparse and transportation was by ox or horse, so slow.

Even the lath was the old split lath. This was the easiest way to get a base to plaster over for interior wall surfaces. In order to accomplish this, a board was sawed very thin, maybe one half inch or less, most likely of elm or another wood that would hang together when it was being split, producing narrow strips of wood that could be positioned with spaces between for the wet plaster to squeeze into.

Patrick Lamb not only needed to clear some land to grow hay and crops for his livestock, but also to provide his family with all the food they consumed. The house construction must have taken second place to these necessities.

Back to the picture and the 1930s; on the right side of the picture is the front of the outhouse that was replaced with the installation of an indoor toilet and plumbing in the mid 1930s. The corner of a chicken house roof is in view next to the outhouse.

There is a story told of when the house was first built. They would at night keep their few sheep in the front hall. The sheep needed to be protected from wild predatory animals and the house was the only safe place they had.

Patrick Lamb came from Ireland on a cattle boat, arriving in New York with no worldly possessions and nobody to sponsor him. He needed to immediately find work in order to eat, or he would live as a pauper. He early on got a job teaching Latin. He was fluent in Latin because he had been educated for the priesthood. It was an excellent education, which a poor Irish farm boy just couldn't afford except under very unusual circumstances.

While making the wilderness into a farm Patrick Lamb was appointed as a judge and served quite extensively locally in that capacity. This gave him an opportunity to put his education to good use in this wild and demanding wilderness.

This chunk of wilderness that he chose was allotted to Patrick Lamb in 1787 for surveying work he had done. He taught school in the winter, but had the summers free and used this to do surveying work for landowners, many of whom owned thousands of acres.

He settled this land and the larger parcel has been continually owned by a descendent of his except when Theron L. St. John owned it after inheriting it from his first wife, Susan Abigail Lamb. Theron soon married Ella Lamb, the niece of his first wife.

It is said that Aunt Ella married Theron to get the farm back in the family. In 1928, upon the death of Theron St. John, the farm then became Ella's, which she continued to operate for about another year with Edward Lamb Nichols' help.

In the spring of 1929 arrangements were made for Ed to purchase the farm from his Aunt Ella. Ed and Letha purchased the farm the month they were married. Four months later the stock market crashed and the Great Depression began.

When Ed and Letha Nichols purchased the farm from his Aunt Ella Lamb St. John, it was the first time in the history of the Lamb farm that the ownership had changed hands as a normal sale with a mortgage as consideration in lieu of cash. This sale included everything. In addition to the real estate, about three hundred acres with the buildings, all the personal property was included. The Lamb farm prior to this had always been transferred from one generation to the next as an inheritance.

The family in an earlier generation had split the property between family members to settle a disagreement. It was later combined back into one farm, but had two deeds because of this. Each deed included more than one lot or parcel of surveyed land.

Early in the Depression the smaller part of the farm with the smaller second house and a hay barn was sold in order to keep ahead of the mortgage payments. The purchaser, Charley Thorington, added a cow stable onto the barn. At the end of World War II, Ed purchased the property back from Charley Thorington when Charley decided to sell and move.

Ed as a child had lived in this smaller of the houses for a while with his mother Sara Lamb Nichols before or at about the time he started school. Part of this time, his father Bryon worked on the farm helping to run it. Bryon soon went into the ministry and the family not long after that moved with him to his new parish.

It was a struggle for Ed and Letha to make ends meet on the farm during the early years of their marriage. This was a time when the Lamb farm was in jeopardy of being lost to the family. They both worked very hard and spent almost no money on themselves.

The farm then was a typical small dairy farm. There were twenty-eight milking cows and one bull. These cows were milked by hand twice a day, seven days a week. There were three people to milk these cows, Ed, Letha, and a hired man. It would take them about two hours at each end of the day depending on circumstances.

There were two or three horses, some pigs and chickens to take care of and work with. Sheep were tried for a few years and so was a hive of bees.

The dairy barn on the Lamb farm wasn't the greatest. The first part consisted of a hay barn about twenty-four feet wide and forty feet long that was well built with large hewn beams. It had been moved from another location on the farm. They then added another, not too well-built section onto it of about the same size with about the same framing, which made a hay barn eighty-six feet long with six bays. The cow stable part was a lean-to addition along the west side of the hay barn, again eighty-six feet long. About four feet on the west side of the hay mow part was utilized as a manger and had a concrete floor. All the rest of the mow had a dirt floor.

The ceiling over the cow stable was made of six-inch round poles placed about two feet apart with lapping rough boards laid on top of them. On top of the boards was a foot of hay to keep the stable warm. It did a good job. This lean-to stable was further added onto in the 1930s, giving it an additional six feet of width. This floor space made room for a second row of cows and young stock. The existing stable was changed some, mostly by using a narrow driveway. There was then no longer a wall to tie calves along. It was a comfortable warm barn and accommodated the cows and young stock nicely, but it took a little extra labor as the hay had to be dragged across the driveway to feed the second row of cows. The Lamb farm was gradually becoming more of a commercial operation in spite of poor buildings.

The farm was also becoming more mechanized through the 1930s. Less hand labor was needed as milking machines powered by a gas engine were used; then, in 1939, electricity was available from the power grid. Prior to this, for two or three years, the farm had utilized a 32-volt Delco system to run a limited number of lights, a clothes washer, and a refrigerator. A rubber-tired farm tractor was added in 1941 and by 1948 horses were no longer used to do much of the farm work.

In the 1950s a three-story 3,000 square foot hen house was built by family labor. It was soon changed to house cows and after a fire, it was remodeled into a more conventional barn. This is the only dairy barn on the farm today.

By the 1960s the herd size had grown to seventy milking cows plus all the young stock needed for replacements. A milking parlor was built and used for efficiency, plus machinery was purchased to help with the field work. Land was rented and hay purchased to feed this large a dairy.

In the 1970s the cattle were sold off and there was a period of time when no milk was produced on the farm. Then Gwen Nichols married and she and her husband, Paul Deysenroth, decided to start farming with dairy cows again.

After the turn of the next century (2000), a cheese plant was built so the family could manufacture on the farm. The cheese made from their own milk supply is retailed on the farm as well as sold to wholesale outlets. Whole raw milk and eggs are sold along with the cheese. These home-grown products, along with baked goods made locally by others, attract many customers to the farm daily.

Gwen and Paul raised three boys and the youngest is now living in the small house with his family, and as of 2020 is an integral part of this farming business.

In 1939 and through the 1940s electricity, along with more modern machinery, changed the way things were done very rapidly in and around the barn as well as the house. This modernization trend has continued and is even accelerating to this day.

Patrick Lamb would not believe the way the farm looks and is operated today.

With Patrick Lamb as generation one, this farm has progressed through two other family surnames until now, six-year-old James Deysenroth

James, Charlotte, Elaina, and Elsie
with their parents, Sami and Dennis Deysenroth

and his three sisters are growing up on the old Lamb homestead as generation nine.

Patrick Lamb's progeny, as they go about their daily lives of school and play on the farm, have no way of coming close to comprehending what life must have been like for Patrick Lamb, his wife Susannah, their 3-year-old son, Edmond, and their 1-year-old daughter, Prudence, living in a log cabin right here on this farm back on New Year's Day when the calendar turned from the year of our Lord, 1799 to 1800.

Sledding

Late 1930s

The ice was good, but not for cutting and storing or for fishing. These activities would only be done on the river or ice pond. This ice was on the brook, a very small stream that when the flow was normal could be easily jumped across in most places, especially as there was a never-ending number of rocks of all sizes and shapes in the brook. These lay along each side as well as in the center of the stream where some would be partially sticking up out of the water in every direction imaginable. This cold December day they were sticking up out of the ice.

My brother Howard and I had each got a new sled from Santa Claus the Christmas before and we devised any system to be able to use them. They were beauties, thirty-six inches long and were the most modern flexible ones made. This may not have been totally true, but close, and we took a lot of pride in them. There was absolutely no rust allowed on the runners that might slow us up ever so much, and because they were flexible, our sleds could be steered or turned quite sharply, especially when you leaned or shifted your weight at exactly the right time.

My father and our hired man were cutting wood for our kitchen stove beside the brook on a two- or three-acre mostly-level spot that we called the wood pile lot. This is not where the trees were cut, that was higher up on the mountain. This lot was cleared pasture and was actually the skid pile where the logs were cut into twelve- to fourteen-inch lengths. These chunks were then split into slabs with a go-devil, and then with an ax the slabs were split into sticks that would go into the stove easily. The process of splitting the wood into small enough pieces to burn changed depending on how big around the log was to start with, and in most cases, how easily the chunk split.

Even the type of saw used was different for different size logs. For the smaller ones a buzz saw was used. This was a circular saw, thirty to thirty-six inches in diameter, mounted on a frame with a rolling table that the logs were laid on; the log was then pushed into the saw. The buzz saw was used for pole wood and anything small, maybe up to twelve inches in diameter. Most years this was the only size cut. Much of this wood was in small enough sizes for two men to lift or roll up a ramp onto the thirty-inch-high saw table. Sometimes neighbors would work together so that three or four did the lifting.

The other common type of saw was a drag saw. It was used to cut logs of larger sizes into splittable and burnable lengths. With a drag saw the logs in larger diameters, also usually much longer, twenty-five feet or so in length, were pulled close, then rolled onto a twelve-inch-high pulley-type cradle on the saw end and onto a track-mounted cart or dolly on the other end. A man could ratchet the log forward twelve or fourteen inches each time he wanted to saw off another block. The saw blade was about four feet long and heavy enough so that when the blade was lowered down on top of the log and the motor-driven pitman pulled it back and forth, it would cut down through the log. This saw was much slower than the buzz saw, but only took one man to operate. It was quite efficient, as he could have time to split the previous chunk into slabs and load the slab into the wagon box. The slabbing was done in the woodpile lot, the fine splitting was done by the wood house.

We completely stopped burning wood when I was about ten so I was always too small to really get involved in a process that was and still is considered dangerous. No matter how many times I asked to help there was little that I was allowed to do. The axes were sharp, the buzz saw was treacherous and the logs would roll while being pulled by a team of horses and could pin you or break a leg easily. I did a lot of watching from a safe distance and was allowed to play nearby, but needless to say I, as any good farm boy would, kept good track of things so I knew how it was done.

My brother Howard and I were using this opportunity to try out the sledding on the brook that actually formed the eastern boundary of the wood pile lot. We would sleigh ride wherever the sleds would go the fastest and furthest. We had at one time or another tried sleigh riding on ice where it was formed from spring runs bubbling up, spreading out and freezing, or where wagon tracks would divert water from any small ditch. Better yet was where a ditch would freeze itself full and then spread out over large uncharted areas. We were even known to carry pails of water to improve the sledding on the tramped path in the snow that led up to our neighbor's barn. Whenever conditions were favorable we would try the sledding anywhere; this included on the brook as it wandered for a half mile or more down through the middle of our farm. Only on rare occasions would it prove to be good enough for us to spend much time sledding in one spot. I think we often spent as much time looking as sledding.

Brook sledding required at least three or four days of good cold weather with very little snow. The temperatures needed to be well below zero at night and no higher than twenty during the day. It was flowing water and water on the move doesn't freeze good. This was also true of ditches and spring runs. Besides, spring water comes from deep in the earth so the temperature and quality changes very little from winter to summer. Deep ground temperatures for us would be around fifty.

Ed Nichols (left) and Howard Nichols on their old sleds

The hallmark of a good spring was if it continued flowing in drought conditions. All the water we used on the farm, including the water for the livestock, came from one spring.

There was often good ice on the ice pond as it was not flowing water, except at the one corner where it entered and exited but level ice did not make good sledding unless you could get a good start and could coast where it was level.

Snow was often your enemy when trying to ice sled. Deep snow would slow you up, hide the stones, and stop you as your sled would sink down into the snow. You didn't want to plow snow, but ride on top of it. With a blanket of snow, ice wouldn't form as quickly. Also, snow falling when ice was forming could make it weak or soft.

We were looking for more sledding opportunities and decided to make a sled out of an old pair of kid skis. The hope was to make it work in soft, deeper snow. The plan: Put two blocks on each ski, put a small board across from one ski to the other then put a wide pine board on top to sit on. Not sure, but I think we must have had help. We ended up with a sled about six inches high, twelve inches wide and maybe five feet long. It worked good, almost. It would go good through deeper snow as it had six inches of clearance and was riding on three-inch-wide runners. Four kids could ride on it at once, but on this sled we sat up.

We never figured out how to steer it; all we could do was aim it. That really was not a problem as we stayed away from obstacles and never tried to come down a hill and go through a gate. Our favorite spot was up by the corner where it was steep near the road, then leveled a little at the bottom by the pond. It worked good as long as the snow wasn't too fast or the pond was frozen. One day we didn't stop before we got to the pond and the ice didn't hold. That water was awful cold to sit in.

Back to our new Santa sleds and brook ice. Just a light dusting of snow could hide a rock that didn't have ice frozen over it. Sometimes there would be a little spray or splashing water that would coat a stone and the runners would go over it very nicely as long as the sleigh runner didn't crack the ice off the rock. Even a pebble the size of a pea would stop you dead in your tracks.

Open water was usually not a problem if we had cold enough weather. Where the ice would freeze it was usually quite thick, but where there was a current or flowing water it would stay open, unfrozen. The open water was likely a foot or foot and half wide. The sleds were long enough to bridge over the open water and keep on going. If the open water was wide then enough momentum or speed was necessary to bridge the open water quickly.

Where water was cascading down from one elevation to the next, it often caused a splashing or spray and hopefully the rocks on one side or the other would ice over and sleds could keep going. These were the spots that most often interrupted our getting a long ride.

Open water was not dangerous as seldom was it even six inches deep. Open water was wet, though, and if we got wet our sleigh riding was most likely over for the day. By the time we got to the house, got dry clothes on and got warm, we would not have time to walk back up the brook. Once wet, you would get cold very quickly.

To get a ride of any appreciable distance it was necessary to lay out the trip carefully. By picking out a starting spot just below an obstruction, taking hold of your sled by gripping both side rails and making a three- to six-foot run before dropping down on the sled, you could start with some momentum. It was always best to lie on your stomach, centered on your sled, so as to balance; then you would have as much control as possible. Sitting up on your sled was for old people and girls, and it really didn't work very good. Once started it was necessary to remember the plan.

The plan today called for gliding over the first eight to ten feet on the almost level ice, moving to the hill road side as you went to avoid bare rocks on the woodpile side, then dropping down ten to twelve inches on ice that had formed when the water cascaded over the rocks. Here you picked up speed and needed to steer your sled sharply left toward the woodpile lot while still descending. Coming up, there was a big rock on the right, all the way to the open water, that we had to go around. We traveled on the ice that was good on the left or woodpile lot side for maybe fifteen feet until just before another drop in elevation. Where it changed elevations only the right side was good again, but we had to cross open water after the big rock to get there. It was only a ten- to twelve-inch gap in the ice so we didn't even have to go across it very straight. You just needed to shift your weight a little and have adequate speed to make this crossing. Then down over this next six-inch-high frozen waterfall to a ten-foot-long level stretch. And so it went.

Waiting for snow, PHOTO BY RAY BRIZZI

Laying out a path that would let you keep on going is where we derived much of our pleasure and on this cold December day we were having good luck, probably the best we had ever had. It wasn't very often when conditions were right to make for good sledding on the brook and we didn't have to go to school.

It seemed like we had been sledding only a few minutes when it was time for the men to quit cutting wood and go back to the barn to do chores and eat supper. We could catch a ride on top of the load of wood and let the horses pull us home. We were tired, cold and hungry, but most likely not wet because if we had gotten wet we would have had to walk home right then. It was necessary to respect the cold and dress accordingly and keep yourself dry.

This was during the Depression times and we had almost no money, but somehow Mom had enough warm clothes for us so we could enjoy outdoor activities.

Living on a farm meant that two sets of clothes were a necessity as our barn clothes could not be worn to school or church and vice versa. We were quite conscious about changing when we got home from school or whenever it was necessary.

When we were small, shoes and arctics (boots) were common attire as footwear for us as it was for all the kids we knew. Your shoes would stay dry as long as we didn't get into water too deep. They buckled tight around your pants or leggings for protection when walking in deep snow. I think with our sledding activities we walked many times the distance we actually rode on a sled. No ski lifts or mechanical transportation. The closest we came was riding on a load of firewood pulled by a team of horses.

Harvesting Ice

1938

I was eight years old and loved helping on the farm. Unfortunately, going to school was more important than helping with the ice harvesting, at least that is how those making the rules saw it. There had been cold nights and cold crisp days with little snow. Ideal weather to freeze ice, for cutting the ice and filling the ice house.

But it was Wednesday and by the time Saturday came the ice house would be full. Fortunately, pink eye was going around so with a few eye rubs ahead of time, which caused some reddening, it was decided to let me stay home. In 1938 there was no antibiotic for pink eye, so kids were kept home so it wouldn't spread. I wasn't sure if anybody really thought it was pink eye or not, but I did get to stay home from school. It couldn't have worked out any better. No restrictions on staying in the house with pink eye, it was an affliction made to order for me. Cutting ice was fun!

Ice was needed on the farm to get the milk cool, then keep it cool until taken to the creamery. Ice could be purchased from the creamery, but that was expensive and we needed to save money if we could. The ice houses would keep the ice that we harvested in the winter through to the warmer summer months. When my dad purchased the farm in 1929, it had an ice house located across the road from the pond, and a fair distance from the milk house. It was far enough away from the pond so that a long sleigh was used to transport the ice from the pond to the ice house, so it could then be pulled up into storage.

Filling the old ice house was a difficult task that required two teams or at least three horses, and five to seven men to get it done efficiently. Farmers would get together and form ice harvesting gangs.

When our ice was needed in the summer each ice cake was dropped out of the ice house, one every two or three days, depending on how hot the days were, then loaded on a steel-wheeled, wooden wheelbarrow, and rolled six hundred feet up to the milk house. Up being the operative word. Uphill is ten times harder than downhill.

Now, in 1936 Dad had the insight to build a new ice house only a few feet away from the edge of the pond, which was right in the middle of the barn yard. This was downhill to the milk house, eliminating the time and energy required with the old ice house. Two men could put ice up, but three were better with the new ice house, and one horse handled the job easily. The need for a big

Ice being moved into storage, Bob Wyer photograph, Courtesy of the Delaware County Historical Association

crew was eliminated. This is where I got a chance to participate; I was the third man.

With the new ice house close to the pond a wooden chute was built about thirty inches wide, and sixteen feet long, reaching from pond to house. This enabled the ice to be pulled directly from the water, up the chute and into the ice house much easier than hauling it on the sleigh. It was one less step which saved a lot of man labor.

The one place I could actually help was in getting the ice up the chute. Only being eight, I couldn't do too much, but I could lead Prince and he did the work.

For the process of moving the ice up the chute we used one horse. For almost everything you did

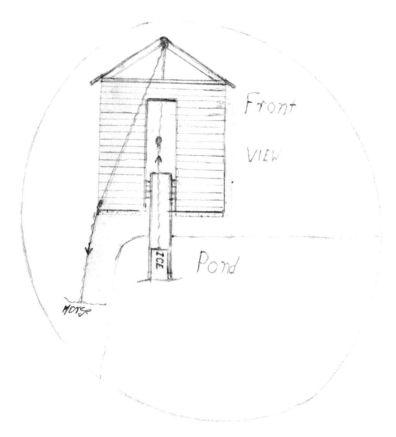

Ice house drawings by Ed Nichols, Jr.

on the farm you used a team of horses, except when harvesting the ice and cultivating the corn. A singletree was needed to hook him up to the rope and a single set of reins to steer the horse, or I would lead him with a short strap attached to his bit.

No one had figured out how to get a horse to push like a bulldozer, so ice was pulled with a rope that went through a series of pulleys. There would be three, maybe four pulleys used when the ice house was near full. That system worked

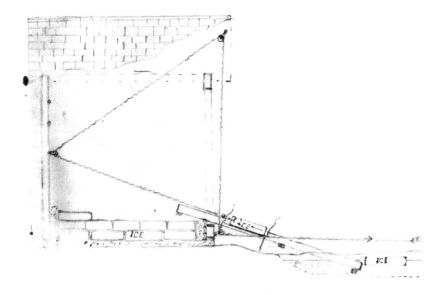

good to get the ice up the chute and back into the ice house.

A strong hay rope made out of hemp was used. It was the size around of a quarter and strong enough that a horse couldn't break it if something caught. The rope would go from the horse's singletree through the first pulley near the ground at the front of the ice house. Then up through the pulley located at the very peak of the ice house, then into, and across to the back of the ice house to a pulley that would line up with where the ice was being placed.

The position of the last pulley was changed as the ice house filled. The rope went from there in a straight line down the chute to the ice pond where it was tied to a set of double-pronged ice tongs made just for this job. Now, ice tongs were unique, with a set of sharp prongs or teeth on each side that would jab into the ice and hold it while the ice cake was being pulled. On the top end there was a chain with a ring in the middle so when you pulled on it, the two sides would come together causing a scissor action to grip the ice cake.

My job was leading Prince. I kept my feet out of the way while leading Prince. He wouldn't intentionally step on me, but if I was in the way when he was pulling all bets were off. He had a job to do.

When there were only two men harvesting, one man would be in the ice house unhooking the tongs from the ice cake they had just pulled up. He would then slide the tongs back down the chute where the ground man would bring Prince back to starting position. He would then grab the tongs and position them on the next block, trying to get the prongs where they would stay until the horse could be moved, thus tightening up the tongs and gripping the ice cake. It was much easier with a third person who could lead the horse while the man near the pond could keep the tongs tight by hand, thus preventing the tongs from slipping off the ice.

In order to get the blocks of ice, the pond had to be sliced in strips. This was done one strip at a time, with Prince pulling an ice plow. The ice plow was special, made from a solid piece of metal three-eighths of an inch thick, eight inches wide and four to five feet long with handles like a regular plow. The ice plow had four sharpened teeth on the bottom and a wide slanted slot in front of the teeth, so the ice shavings would come to the top of the groove and not plug it up.

The ice plow scored a thin groove in the ice a little deeper each time you went over it. It took three or more times to get the groove deep enough so the ice would break off. There was an arm on one side used as a guide, making the strip of ice a constant width.

The first time the horse could be in front of the plow. As the groove got deeper the horse had to be hooked off to the side, far enough so that he would be walking on solid ice. The pond was two feet deep, presenting no real danger like the larger ponds, but we were careful just the same.

Once the groove was cut deep enough, the two foot strip of ice the length of the pond was broken off. Then it was cut into blocks.

For chopping the strips into blocks we used a spud. It was a six-inch square piece of metal about an eighth of an inch thick with five sharp diamond shaped points across the end. A four foot wooden handle was attached like a shovel. By chopping the points into the ice several times in a line across the strip, it could be broken off. Don't hit your toe, because your boots would be ruined and it would be painful.

I wasn't strong or quick enough to chop the block off, and by the time I was, we no longer had a need to cut ice.

There was another tool that I could use, the ice pick. This was a long wooden-handled tool that

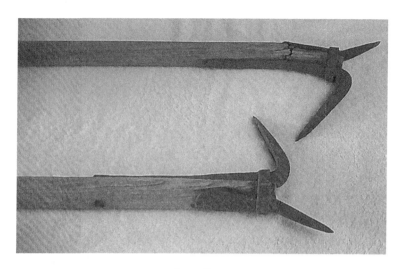

Ice pikes

had two steel points, each pointing in the opposite direction, like a song my father liked about Hortense who had two teeth in her mouth, one pointed north, and the other pointed south.

The one point was positioned so that it could be jabbed into the ice cake and pushed away. The other point curved like a hook backward so you could pull the ice towards you. We had two ice picks, one long-handled, and one short-handled.

The long-handled one was used when the ice chunks were further out in the water. By pushing or pulling, you could get it to go where you needed it. Almost as good as playing video games.

Pushing, pulling, and moving the ice in the open water to where it could be hooked with the tongs took skill. I thought it was a blast trying to maneuver the ice around. Once the pond had some ice cut off of it, so there weren't channels or hallways that the ice had to follow, it became more fun. I did not have an opportunity to float the ice, only the first few, as I was leading the horse and was occupied. My father, the ground man, would be able to float the last of the recently cut chunks to the base of the chute so he could hook the tongs on them.

All the ice was packed in sawdust with a layer of sawdust between each layer of ice. It had to be capped off with mounds of sawdust so that it would not melt too much.

As a child of eight, I had had a ball. I loved working on the ice harvesting with my dad.

I wonder if my helping was a net gain for them; doubt it.

Too bad pink eye only lasted one day. Guess I forgot to rub my eye.

Banking the House

Circa 1936

This was going to be a fun day. Almost all the interesting things happened on a school day when I couldn't go with the men. I had started going to school, and it didn't take long for me to realize that going to school wasn't all it was cracked up to be.

I was sure going to miss things like cutting ice, riding up to the woodpile and back, helping a neighbor, and watching Dad working on building projects or equipment repairs, plus many other interesting things. Even the routine winter chores were fun to watch and help with. Many times I knew quite well what needed to be done, I just wasn't yet big enough to do the job. Guess that is what made it fun.

Excuses, always excuses; couldn't cut ice, the weather had to be right. It had to be cold enough long enough to freeze ice, but then nice enough to work outdoors. The wood had all been hauled down from the woodpile, so no more wagon rides up and back. No neighbors needed help doing some interesting project. And the final straw, we had to go to town to get a haircut. Doggone haircuts anyway.

But today I lucked out; it was Saturday and a nice early fall day. Dad mentioned at breakfast that they were going to bank the house for winter. There would be a few things I could do. I would more likely be a hindrance than a help, but I was never made aware of it.

Mid morning, after the usual chores were done, the team was unhooked from the manure wagon and hooked onto the utility wagon. This was nothing more than an old manure box that had seen better days, with an old steel-wheeled wagon under it. Wagons and the boxes, hay racks, and special riggings for logs or lumber or stone were all made to be interchangeable.

A steel-wheeled wagon could be a hazard to your health. Not so much in getting run over by it, but the jarring you sustained while riding in it.

The worst was traveling up the cattle lane in that old wagon. Here the soft soil had been eroded away for many years. This was bad because of the thousands of time that cows' hooves had trampled on it, killing the grass and loosening the soil. Sometimes the ride was so rough the men would actually walk, not ride. None of the other wagon roads were all rocks like the lane was. Most were quite smooth when compared to the lane.

On this Saturday we would be going in the other direction, not up the lane, so our ride would be quite smooth and enjoyable.

First, the men picked up a crow bar and a post mall, then drove down back behind the old chicken house and picked up some posts and some wide pine boards that were kept for this purpose. They took them out on the west side of the house. They set the posts in the ground, spacing them just under the length of the boards they had picked up and about six inches from the house. The posts were set by punching a hole in the ground with the bar and then pounding the posts into the hole with the mall.

These posts were not 5'6" long like Dad made his fence posts, but shorter. Some may have been old cherry fence posts that had rotted off, and been resharpened, but I think they were mostly pine, not cherry. Pine was much easier to pound a nail into and much easier to pull it out the next spring. Dad had a plentiful supply of pine to split posts out of, so that was the logical way to go.

The boards were nailed onto the posts, one above the other, high enough to come up to the top of the stone foundation. This created a solid wall, but not a smooth wall. It was the length of the west side of the house and across part of the front.

Down in back by the old potato cellar, Dad had kept a pile of pine needles from last year. The wagon was filled with those needles by using a dun fork or ensilage fork. They were then pitched into the space between the just made board wall and the stone foundation of the house. The house foundation was a field stone wall, tightly laid and

Our insulating material

mostly plastered, but it leaked air. Banking was my father's system to keep the cellar warmer. There was no furnace in the cellar, just stoves upstairs, so the basement and the floors of the house could get cold, very cold.

Now for me comes the fun part. Because some of the pine needles were lost each year the men would take the empty wagon down into the pines and by using dun forks, scrape the pine needles up into piles and then pitch them into the wagon. The pine grove at that time was almost one hundred percent pine and quite thick, so harvesting pine needles was an easy task. This was a very inexpensive way of shielding the foundation wall, but not a very permanent one.

Riding on top of those needles was the best part. That ride would have been quite comfortable even if we had gone up the lane.

A big coal-fired furnace was later installed and the practice of banking the house was soon abandoned.

No more rides down into the pines on a nice fall day to scrape needles into piles and to smell the aromatic pine fragrance. Riding on top of the needles going back to the house was our Cadillac ride. This ride had a purpose other than just the ride. Not like getting a ride at the fair where you buy a ticket to go nowhere to get absolutely nothing.

The needles did prick once in a while as needles will do, but it still was an enjoyable ride, a ride to remember.

Half Walking

1938–1944

Ned was getting old and my father had decided to semi-retire him. He was over twenty, which is old for a horse, and we depended on him as one half of the team to carry the full load of our farm work. He had been part of the team longer than I had been alive.

The team worked together hour after hour with Ned on the left and Prince on the right. They were stabled in the same order. He was the horse in the middle stall with Prince on the right, next to the outside wall. There was a third empty stall to the left of Ned that was utilized as a temporary pig pen some of the time. This stall would soon be Ned's stall.

The average farmer was not a big or avid horse trader. There were, however, three farmers nearby who made a living mainly by trading horses and cattle. Bill Ceas was an older man who retired in the mid-1940s. His barn was in the middle of Bloomville, a village about two miles west of us.

Prince and Ned waiting to go in the barn

The other two were brothers, Ed and John Foote, who were eight miles east of us and owned adjacent farms just west of Hobart. They remained in business until about 1960. Ed Foote's dispersal auction was in March of 1960. They came into their own right after WWII when farmers were mechanizing their operations. They both, because of this mechanizing trend, changed and grew into machinery dealerships. Their ability to take cattle or horses in on trade for machinery, which they did very often, was a big advantage for them. They were willing to dicker almost anything, for almost anything, and often did.

I remember going with Dad to Ed Foote's in Hobart, who had by far the largest business of the three, to look at horses. Guess Dad looked at over twenty horses there that day, but apparently didn't see one he liked or wanted. It may have been too much money. What I do remember about that day was walking behind a row of ten to twelve horses. The walkway behind them was no wider than three or three and a half feet wide. All I could think about was if they kick, my face would be just the right level. Sure hope they were not sharp-shod. They were stomping around a little as they were just being fed hay. Boy, was I glad to get out of there.

These three local dealers, plus many others scattered all over the rural areas of the northeast, would go out west to the corn belt or wheat country and purchase horses by the carload. I don't know if the dealers ever revealed where the horses came from and am sure some were unbroken. Were they obtained through auctions, or direct from the crop farmers or through the services of an agent? We were told the crop farmers felt that a horse over six to eight years old was too old to work all day, steadily pulling a plow or disk.

Our local dealers would buy the horses, ship them east by rail, and sell them to the local dairy farmers. Those that came in unbroken or wild would need to be tamed and broken.

Supposedly you could look in a horse's mouth at their teeth and tell within a year how old they were. Thus the saying "don't look a gift horse in the mouth." I always had my doubts about how accurate the system was. I am sure it was far more accurate when the horse was young than when they got to be, say, fifteen. Were the horses that Bill Ceas had for sale just seven or eight, or maybe ten plus?

Dad purchased from Bill Ceas a big bay horse we called Turk that got the center stall and became the left horse in the team with Prince. He seemed to work in fine, but after a couple of weeks Dad had the vet come and look at him. Our veterinary, Dr. Dickson, also did Bill Ceas's veterinary work and could have a conflict of interest. He looked the horse all over and came over to Dad and said "I think this horse needs to be traded." Nothing more was said. To this day I do not know what the concern was on my dad's part or what the real diagnosis was. Now begs the question: Who is going to end up finally taking the big loss on this flawed merchandise? How many times will he be traded?

Dad traded Turk back to Bill Ceas for a bay mare that we called Judy. I do not know if there was any kind of a warranty with Turk. I doubt it and I do not know how much money changed hands either time. I am quite sure that if it hadn't been to my father's financial advantage to trade the second time with Ceas he would have traded horses elsewhere.

Judy was just a little bigger than Prince. She seemed to be just a bit clumsy, but it never bothered and she worked in just fine with Prince. When we stopped using horses on the farm Judy was sold or traded, but Prince, who was getting quite old, was kept and died of natural causes.

Even though she was a big equine, Dad was sure Judy was part mustang. The first thing after getting them hooked together each day they would be driven to an outside watering trough. One day in the winter Judy reared up on her hind legs and brought her front feet down through the ice on the watering trough before the ice could be chopped. She may have seen this done or more likely she may, if she was part mustang, have inherited that impulse. Mustangs would inherently know how to get a drink of water if a stream was frozen over. No matter, be on guard when chopping the ice for the horses to get a drink.

We now had three work horses. The big team and old Ned, the little smaller, most likely part Morgan, that now occupied the far left stall.

Ned's main purpose was pulling the dump rake in haying. It was my job to rake up the scatterings of hay, which took forever sometimes. At least it seemed that way. When raking fields near the barn Ned could move right along when headed toward the barn, but plodded miserably slow when going away from the barn. This was very noticeable and quite frustrating at times. Slapping the end of the horse nearest to you with the reins didn't help much. Maybe I didn't do it hard enough; maybe I didn't want to.

We could ride old Ned almost any time we wished unless he had been working and deserved his rest. We did not always have a saddle and could ride him if we could get on. Before I had reached the ripe old age of ten the horse was quite tall and my legs kind of short. That changed very slowly.

No saddle, no stirrup, no can get on without a struggle.

Getting on did get easier as we got older and bigger. But as we got older, Ned got older and he would stop and rest more often like many of our grandfathers seemed to do. As we got so we could enjoy a horseback ride more, Ned was going downhill and needed to be pampered more.

The best laid plans of mice and men, which includes boys, didn't seem to work with old Ned. Early on we thought we could use the milk block for getting on. The milk block was about the same level as a stirrup which should work fine. That did work the first time, then Ned took care of that. The first time I led Ned right close to the milk block, he came right alongside very nicely and Howard jumped on. Staying on was a little tricky with nothing but Ned's mane to grab hold of. Practice would be helpful.

When my turn came it didn't go so good. When Howard led Ned close by the milk block his head was nice and close but his tail end wasn't. The miserable old beast was walking

(L. to R.) Ed Nichols, cousin Jim Nichols, Howard Nichols, with cousin Ricky Richmond riding Ned

sidewise just enough so there was no way I could jump on. Leading him by several times in both directions just gave him a chance to practice his sidestepping with his hind legs. Either direction, his body was far enough away from the milk block so I could not get on. He could side step left or he could side step right with equal efficiency.

When we were quite small it was hard to tell who controlled whom. Ned would stop and eat the grass if he got on the lawn. We tried in earnest not to let him. His head would go down. He would start eating and we could not keep him walking. Whoever was riding just had to set up there and complain, and if one of us was leading we had to pull hard enough to get him to move. Maybe we could turn this to our advantage.

Maybe we could have him lift us up, kind of like getting on a camel.

OK, why not! The next time we took Ned out for a ride we started on the lawn. I held the lines and Howard quickly got astraddle of his neck. His head went up; Howard was on like a clown in a circus, backward. Not the best system, now what do you do. How do you get turned around?

Ned was very clever and always seemed to make the best of a situation for himself. He would never hurt either one of us boys on purpose, nor the men, I'm sure. I just think he didn't want those two little squirts riding him.

Before my father had purchased the third horse, Ned was still used as one of the team. The horses were always shod but it was different in the summer than in the winter. I think the rear feet always had just plates or at most mud corks put into the plates. (We always called these additions to horseshoes corks, although I've learned that elsewhere they were called caulks or studs.)

It got so that you could purchase horseshoes that had cork-like bars made right on the shoe. I know Dad used them a lot in the later years. The old style plates had four holes in them. The two in the front were closer together than the two in the back. Corks like blunt pegs could be pounded into the hole. They would dig in just a little in softer surfaces so the horse could pull better. My father never wanted much of a cork on the hind feet because if a horse was surprised and kicked, it could be quite damaging.

The front shoes were different. They could safely have sharp corks or ice corks put in them. These corks would have a sharp wedge-like point the size of a quarter protruding below the plate. They looked dangerous and could have been if a person was stepped on by one of them. The weight of the horse would drive the points down into the ice or frozen ground and keep the horse's foot from slipping. With sharp corks just on the front feet a horse could walk on slippery ice better that a man could.

One winter the little stream that crossed our lane had frozen full and caused the lane to flood and be covered with a solid sheet of ice. The lane had to be traversed to bring wood down from the wood pile. Ned, when walking on that sheet of ice, would walk with his front feet and slide his plated hind feet along. Ned was half walking, just the front half.

Sand Castles for Keeps

1935–1946

I have never built a sand castle out of sand. Not that I remember. The only opportunity I would have had was the few days that our family spent in New Jersey at my aunt's and uncle's when I was about six. We spent one day at the Jersey shore with our cousins. If we had made a sand castle, it would have been mostly imaginary, like most six-year-old's sand castles are. I think I was more interested in watching my father learning to cast a fishing line way, way out in the ocean, far different than fishing at home. We did not have fish for supper.

We had a sand box at home but the sand was not the same. It would not hold a form or shape good. It wouldn't even come close to holding a vertical or plumb surface. Even when wet, the face of a pile of sand couldn't be made much steeper than two inches high for every one inch of sidewise measurement. There was foundry sand in a town near us, but we really weren't interested in sand castles. The things that my father built on our farm were much more interesting and way more practical.

Our sand box was mostly a landscaping project, roads for our little cars or tractors, or a hill to climb, or ditches to get stuck in. Maybe even get an imaginary load of hay to tip over.

Building things out of sand wasn't my favorite pastime anyway; it was just something to do when there wasn't something more interesting going on, like my father building things, real things. I'm not sure if I did have a favorite pastime. Living on a farm there was usually, not always, but usually, many things to do, or watch being done and I took advantage of all that I could. I'm sure that many times my father or the hired man would wish I'd stay out of their way. Or that at least I couldn't think of so many questions.

Making homemade lawn furniture was a good example. My mother wanted some good lawn furniture to sit on. Dad agreed and decided to make it himself, probably their only option. The chairs and then a bench, which was kind of an afterthought, were made out of leftover materials that were saved from past projects, then stored somewhere around the farm. The nails were the only exception and sometimes even then a nail, when pulled out could be straightened and reused. With the milk price so low there wasn't money to spend unless the item was absolutely necessary.

These lawn furniture pieces couldn't be thrown together just randomly, like sand castles, or designed as you went along. First they needed to fit the posteriors that were going to sit on them. Put in modern day jargon, they needed to comply with certain predetermined design criteria, whatever that was.

I do not remember any of the particulars, but was learning without even being aware that I was learning. First at least a rudimentary plan was needed. By measuring chairs, those that were comfortable, we had a place to begin. The chairs also had to be made out of existing saved materials left over from other projects. More likely though, the materials were gleaned from tearing down all or part of unneeded buildings. Materials available could be a design-limiting factor. The results of that project were two single chairs and one nine-foot-long bench. The bench was by far the simplest, and as it turned out, the most used.

My mother, Letha, sitting on the bench Dad made

It fit people the best, especially us kids. I think the chairs needed cushions. The bench was made out of two nine-feet-long, twelve-inch-wide cherry boards, one for the seat and one for the back. Available old four by four pine studs were used as structural parts for some parts of the bench.

A little later in the decade my father made a rubber-tired wagon. He had acquired a junked model A Ford car and removed the running gear. I do not remember seeing any of the other parts ever setting on our old junk pile, so am unsure what really happened.

The major difficulty would be to make the tongue steer the wagon so that it followed the horses when turning. There was a difference in how this wagon would be steered. With the typical horse-drawn steel-wheeled farm wagon the entire front axle pivoted on a center post. With this axle, as with all standard cars back then, the wheels pivoted on a spindle at each end of a semi-stationary axle. There was a tie rod that went across between them and pivoted both wheels in unison, either left or right. The tongue had to be attached to this tie rod so that as the tongue turned, the tie rod would be moved in the correct direction and the correct distance to steer the wheels. The tongue also had to be attached to the axle so that the horses did all their pulling on the axle, and not on the tie rod.

The system that was devised worked well and the wagon lasted a long time.

The rubber-tired wagon is on the left

This wagon was far superior to the old steel-wheeled wagon in several ways. Rubber tires meant it was so much nicer to ride in. Second, a load of whatever wouldn't be bounced off so quickly and the box was lower to the ground making loading something easier. It was also a lot easier on the horses not having the tongue whip sidewise every time one front wheel or the other dropped in a hole or hit a stone.

I was not involved in the construction of this wagon. I was too small but I did observe it with interest. I could only imagine what it was going to look like and really didn't understand the design problems until after it was built. The only sand castle aspect to building that wagon, it was a product of the mind first.

My father added onto the barn to make another part row of cows with some room for calf pens and an engine room. I suppose this was the cow's castle but I never thought of it that way. It was nothing fancy but comfortable, and made to last. I was still way too young to even conceive of the enormity of this project with Dad's limited assets, but bits and pieces sure did interest me. Every bit of it was done by hand labor by my father and a hired man. It took them a long time as regular farming activities had to be taken care of first.

No blueprints. There were some marks and numbers put on a piece of paper, but darn few. These were just enough calculations to validate some of the critical features and measurements to make the parts fit. It was all designed by my father in his head. The paper was maybe, as I had seen more than once, an old envelope with the three sides cut, then laid flat. The inside was clean for writing on.

First, an eighty-five-foot ditch was dug by hand for the new west wall. Forms were made the old-fashioned way. The lumber was rough sawed (unplaned or sized) and the forms were held together by old baling wire twisted to draw it tight against the spacers.

My father had, or borrowed, an old cement mixer powered by a small gas engine. We did not have electricity yet. I know he owned a mixer some years later and may have owned that one. I remember the pulley wobbling and he re-poured the pulley bearing. He melted old lead pipes to do that. The mixing barrel would hardly hold one cubic foot of concrete at a time, so it took many batches to just pour the wall.

The wall was only six inches thick and sat on a bed of pounded-up rock. Today, new foundation walls are eight inches thick or thicker and set on a poured concrete footer. Today, concrete comes in a big truck and runs down a metal chute into the form. Today, there isn't much incentive to economize on the amount of concrete that is used. Back then every bit of it was shoveled, most likely three times, first to get the sand and gravel, then to mix the concrete, and then to place it in the forms.

The other big concrete task for the addition was the floor. In order to fill in the eighteen-inch deep space up to the same level as the existing floor, you couldn't just call up the local gravel supplier to do it. You harnessed up your horses, hitched them on a wagon and loaded it up with rock from an unneeded stone wall. The stones were all handled by hand and then pounded or cracked up by hand so as to make them solid or firm. This six-foot-wide by eighty-five-foot-long space took many wagon loads of stone to fill up and a lot of pounding with a sledge hammer to get the stone broken up and leveled sufficiently to pour concrete over. The leveling of the finished floor or the sloping of the floor had to be preplanned for proper drainage. The locations of the steel pins or bolts that held the pen posts and stanchions in place had to be pinpointed and set when the concrete was first poured.

I do not remember anything about framing up the walls, constructing the roof, or tearing out the old exterior wall. I must have been in school at that time. I do remember being on the roof one time when they were putting down the tar paper for the roofing. I was also around when some of the pens and stanchions were being built. It took a lot of time to put it all together.

* * *

A nine-year-old boy is asked which would you rather have: A pony or a swimming pool. Wow, what a choice! I had to decide. I think I chose the one that my father least expected. It was quite simple for me at that time. Nobody, but nobody had a swimming pool in their front yard. Today many homes have private swimming pools in their yard. Back then there weren't even very many municipal pools in fairly large towns.

I had learned to swim in a small pool in the brook. The spring-fed brook was always cold and the biggest pool in it wasn't deep enough, so that I touched bottom when dog paddling. I didn't learn to distance swim as there was just one small area that was deep enough. I really wasn't swimming, just staying afloat. We were not allowed to go in the river by ourselves, so swimming there almost never happened.

We didn't lack for a horse to ride on, what we lacked was a saddle to put on the horse. Would a pony be a lot better? Wouldn't we need two ponies? We could ride old Ned most any time we wished, unless he had been working doing the raking and deserved his rest.

It took some time to get the swimming pool built. Again, this project took second place to regular farm activities and it really wasn't easy. I often wondered if Dad had second thoughts.

There was a ditch that ran kind of catty-corner in the space between our lawn and the Thorington line fence. The ditch mainly handled runoff that came under the road from part of the barnyard area. The ditch moved a little west before turning sharp west across Thorington's lane and emptying in the brook. During dry weather the only water in the ditch would have been the overflow from the watering vat. That was a small continuous stream of fresh water from a half-inch pipe. The runoff water would have to run around the built-up pool embankment on the west or brook side. The placement of the pool meant that most of the dirt that had to be dug away was on the deep end toward the house. Other places needed to be dug down a little and very little fill was needed in other places. The pool drain would be located near the west corner of the deep end and empty right into the existing ditch.

Howard and I decided we would start some of the digging. Big joke! The typical way to move dirt for grading purposes was with a horse-drawn pan or scraper. I can't remember what it was called. I think dirt scraper. They undoubtedly had bulldozers, but I had never seen one. Besides, we wouldn't have the money to hire one. Dirt was moved by man power, or horse power, real horse power. We could use the team while the men were milking and doing chores. First, the dirt was loosened up with a plow. Then it was scraped up with the pan, pulled to the dumping spot and the pan was then tipped bottom side up. Now this is all theory. Howard could drive the team well enough, but I was nowhere near big enough to handle a plow or especially the scraper. They both were a task for a good-sized man and it took practice. I'm sure my father realized this, but trying was the best way for me to learn this little fact of life.

The pool was to be fifteen feet wide and thirty feet long. It was to be two feet deep at the shallow end and four feet deep at the deep end. The walls would be six inches thick and the bottom would be two-inch thick concrete poured over a bed of pounded rock. This work was almost entirely done while we were in school. I can recall watching or helping with none of it.

Something that kind of intrigued me was the use of dressed lumber for the inside of the forms for the pool walls. Dad wanted to re-side the wagon house. He decided if he used shiplap siding backward as the forming surfaces, and drilling one-eighth-inch holes for the forming wire to go right through the lap, he could reuse the lumber for his siding. The holes would not likely line up when reused, making the siding a tight seal and any concrete stains would be on the stud side of the siding and never show. It worked and I remember years later seeing the occasional little hole in the wagon house siding just part way through.

The town was hauling gravel out of our gravel bank and they were talked into hauling in enough top soil to fill in around the pool and grade up onto the lawn. It was all left in piles.

Again Howard and I were going to do our part. We worked at leveling off the piles with very little success! This was not sand and we were not building sand castles. We already knew the horse-drawn scraper was out of the question for us, so we set out to use shovels and a wheelbarrow where it needed to be moved some distance. We would have graduated from high school before we got it done. I think the town again came to our rescue and spent an hour or two with their big grader. This whole project was accomplished over like two years.

The problem of getting water into the pool is a new chapter by itself. The pool leaked a little so it had to have fresh water running in all the time.

Brother Denny in the pool Dad built

There was often a crowd at our pool

The first pipe wasn't big enough to keep up, so that was changed a couple of times. The brook had to be dammed up to direct the water into the pipe. We had to use rock and sod. The dam couldn't be made out of sand, it didn't work.

It is surprising what a boy learns about so many things when being confronted with a project like keeping a swimming pool swimmable. You develop an appreciation for what part soil technology, hydraulics, solar radiation, and just so many things play in the simplest of projects.

Of all the choices I have had to make, choosing a swimming pool is one of the better ones.

Not only did Howard and I enjoy many hours in the pool but it was a meeting place for boys from the community to come and have a good time. My bedroom was unofficially designated the changing room and on many a sunny day several swimming suits could be seen on the window sill drying out. There may have been some not taken back home all summer. In fact I think we had loaners. Some fifty years later while visiting with a friend of my youngest brother, he mentioned riding his bike up as a teenager and enjoying swimming in the pool. Denny, my youngest brother, was twelve years my junior so the pool had an extended useful life span; eventually even my children enjoyed the pool. It took a lot of work but created a lot of enjoyment. We knew it wouldn't be washed away with the first big wave that came ashore like sand castles are.

Too Big to Flush

1934–1945

Growing up on a farm puts you in touch with real things, like the death of an animal. All the farm animals we kept were way too big to be flushed down a toilet if they died. Even a chicken was too big. I was five or six when we first got a flush toilet and there would have been no thought of using the toilet for anything but appropriate purposes. Nobody would ever think of flushing even a very small dead pet or mouse down the toilet like you often hear about in these modern times. We had not heard the term food chain, but we understood the principle. Those animals would either be buried or put some place where another animal could use them as food.

There were three different kinds of animals, plus chickens, that we kept to sell or as a food source. The farm dog, "Joe," and some cats were the exceptions. A few sheep were kept for a year or two experimentally. They had little potential for profit, so were sold. Shortly after the sheep we did keep a billy goat for a while, which if you were mean enough to him made a good pet.

The least important of the large farm animals was a brood sow. She provided Dad with some weaned pigs to sell once or twice a year. We did have a second brood sow one year, a young one that replaced the old sow. Keeping pigs was also a way of utilizing milk from freshened cows— those that had just calved. There would be colostrum in the milk from the first few milkings so it could not be sold.

Feeding the pigs wasn't my favorite thing to do. The freshened cow's milk was not fed to the pigs fresh. It was dumped into an old milk can, then meted out over a period of time. It would sour and even form chunks like cheese. When you took the lid off the can to get the allotted amount, it smelled, really smelled. It would knock you on your little fanny even if you held your breath. The pigs loved it.

The idea of raising pigs was to sell the pigs just as soon as they were weaned Any small pig that we raised past weaning was for our own use. I remember just one exception. I think the old brood sow had too many pigs for Dad to sell. I remember the one time the old sow had 13 pigs in one litter. You usually hoped to get close to ten. The more pigs the better, up to a point. This old sow only had twelve nipples. One little pig was out of luck. This did not turn out to be a problem. Almost always in large litters there would be a runt, sometimes two. This little, poorly-developed pig would sometimes be given special care, bottle fed or whatever, but usually it didn't work. They would be dead in a couple of days. Sometimes a sow would eat their own little pig. This sow lost one very quickly. Even when they did live they were at a disadvantage. Once a runt, always a runt. They would have problems competing for their food.

There was no market for more just-weaned pigs that year so Dad raised a couple until they weighed about a hundred pounds liveweight, then butchered them and peddled the halves door to door. I can remember my father putting some butcher's paper on the floor of a homemade utility-type trailer, putting the four pig halves on it, then covering them with more paper. Then a canvas was tied over top. We actually did go door to door, or farm to farm, as the case may be. Dad would weigh each half as it was sold, using an old set of hanging balance scales.

Even a good brood sow eventually ended up as a food source for somebody, most likely us. It was necessary to plan ahead like six months when keeping weaned pigs for your own use.

Cows were different, they were kept for the milk they would produce. But they also would eventually end up as meat on somebody's table. Only the female calves that we wanted to raise as replacements were kept, all other calves were sold when they were a day old, for veal. Cows were sold when they ceased making you a profit or when another cow would make more profit.

Determining that is another story and sentiment should not play a part in that decision. The size of your barn limited you to a maximum number of cows. Most of the animals on farms did not die of natural causes or by accident. Their imminent death was calculated by the owner.

Horses were different. They were more of a working pet, at least those that you had raised or had kept and worked with for a long time. It was easy to become fond of a particular animal, any animal. This was especially true of a horse.

We did our own butchering to provide our family with our own meat. We butchered about one cow, two pigs and some chickens each year. Chickens were butchered as needed. My father did butcher chickens for a local store as they got orders for them. The others animals were done during cold weather so the meat would get cold enough to keep until it was all processed.

There was some preplanning needed for this to happen smoothly. First, my father always believed that an animal that was gaining weight or growing would produce meat that would be tender. Because of this an animal chosen to be slaughtered for our own use would be fed a higher calorie diet for a few weeks ahead of time.

Butchering any large animal was quite a project for the men, but also for my mother, as the meat had to be processed for preservation. Some parts of this fell to her to do. Before 1940, freezing meat by the home owner was not an option. After the availability of home freezers in the forties it was easier, but it still took time to cut up and wrap the meat to be frozen.

When the day came to butcher a cow, some things were ready or handy by. Knives were sharpened, of course. Two sets of tackles were hooked to an overhead beam and a stone boat was pulled close by the haymow doorway. I'm not sure if Mom got canning jars ready or made other preparations. I guess I just never observed those things.

The chosen cow was led out to the ground floor haymow, under where the tackles were hung. This was usually a struggle as our cows were never taught to lead and would fight the rope halter. The cow was hit in the head with a sledge hammer, which would instantly knock her unconscious. Her jugular vein was immediately cut so that all the blood would drain out of her. A set of tackles was hooked to each hind leg and she would be pulled up off the ground so that they could skin her. The skin would be cut loose from the meat starting with the hocks on the hind legs first, and then cut loose all the way down to the ears. The carcass would be hoisted up a little at a time with the tackles as the skin or hide was cut or peeled away. Hoisting her up was no easy task as one had to pull hard on the rope to lift the carcass. This required one man on each tackle set pulling simultaneously.

I'm sure there was a market for the hide but am also sure it was not worth much. We did not attempt to use the hide for anything ourselves.

The cow would be drawn and the innards dropped onto the stone boat. Some of the internal organs can be used for food, but we never did. The stone boat would be pulled by our team of horses up into the pasture and the innards left there. The lower part of the legs and the head would be left there also. Wild animals would smell them and they would be quickly gone. I'm sure the wild animals could smell them as the smell of a freshly opened up carcass was strong and I did not like it. Sometimes I did not care to eat the meat for a few days afterward. Give me another bowl of cereal.

Cutting the carcass up for eating or processing was a task. First it was cut in half from tail end to neck. A meat saw, or more accurately a bone saw, was used where a bone needed to be parted. Then it was quartered, with each quarter, one at a time, taken in the house and placed on the kitchen table to be cut up into whatever. This is when my mother became fully involved. Dad would do the cutting and Mom would take care of the canning or preserving. Canning all the meat that was not smoked or salted down must have been a long, hard process. The vast majority was canned. Later on, after we had a freezer, it was wrapped and frozen in meal-sized portions. Very soon after this, about the time of World War II, the cow would be picked up by truck, taken to a local slaughterhouse and custom butchered. The quarters would be returned to us. Then it soon became customary to have a local meat market pick up the quarters, cut them up, grind some hamburg and freezer wrap all the meat. At first we wrapped our own meat, but that, too, gradually changed. Having the hamburg custom ground also changed during that decade.

Pigs were handled very similarly, with a couple of exceptions. It was almost impossible to lead a pig with a rope, so getting the pig from its pen to the butchering site was a task. Leading them with a bucket of food worked the best. My father had built a crate, sized so that a large pig would just fit in, but getting a pig in it was a chore. It had a vertically-sliding gate on each end so that a pig could be pushed in on one end and then let out the other. It had skids so that it could be slid onto a wagon or truck. It was mainly used to transport a sow over to Elmer Murdoch's farm when Dad wanted a sow bred. Elmer kept quite a few pigs, including a boar. Other farmers would borrow this crate on occasions.

The second difference was, a pig was not skinned, but scalded and the hair scraped off before drawing. The task of getting water hot enough for the scalding process was challenging. Heating the water in an open top steel drum was the typical way. One year my father took some milk cans up to the creamery and had them put their steam hose in each can of water to get it real hot. He covered the cans with a blanket and hurried home to scald the pig. This process worked good and was continued until we started having the pigs custom butchered.

I never remember us being asked the kind of trick question, "where does hamburg come from" or "where does milk come from," expecting us to answer, "from the meat market" or "from a bottle." We grew up knowing very young in life the truth about these things.

Boy Work

Circa 1940

My brother Howard and I had just decided we
wanted to ride in a buggy wagon like the old folks
did before the time of the automobile. But we
were at a disadvantage as buggies weren't very
plentiful and there were a lot less horses to pull
wagons. Not sure the possibility of a buggy ride
had crossed our minds until now.

We didn't come up with the idea out of the
clear blue, we kind of had a prompt. I do not recall how come there was a buggy setting out past
our tool shed right on the bottom edge of a mostly
gently sloping meadow, but there it was. Our father had put it there, we were quite sure, but how
come and where did he get it from? I do not have
any recollection of a buggy stored anywhere
around our place before that time. Where it came
from, I do not know. I don't remember ever seeing
it stored in our shed or in the hay barn, but there
it sat and it was a challenge.

We quite quickly came up with a plan that should work with any luck at all. Our reasoning behind our plan was, we coasted downhill on a sled, why not a buggy? We were imagining the two of us tooling right along down the hill, each hanging on a steering rope, then coming to nice stop, still in the meadow. This was something more we could play with, in our minds something to work at, and although I didn't realize it at the time, something from which to learn. That kind of learning was OK as it wasn't in school, it didn't take me away from something important.

We both knew what school was as Howard was most likely in his first or second or third year of going to school and I was two years bigger. I have no way of dating this caper exactly, but that is close. We were about to get into something new for us and something we weren't quite big enough to tackle, but that didn't matter. It would fall under my father's often used category of "boy work." If something that we boys were involved in didn't work out, or it ended up being disruptive or even a disaster, that is the descriptive term he used. Most of the time it was fairly accurate. Many a time he must have realized the potential for difficulties or danger of an impending caper, but kept his distance. As long as we couldn't get hurt—except for minor injuries—we would learn a lesson. I'm sure Dad understood how a boy's mind worked and it didn't take much of a clue to surmise what was coming. Many a time it was tools or equipment or supplies that the men had been using while doing something along the line of farming that we got to play with when they had to go to do chores. If what we were using or playing with was damaged, we were made to understand that nobody wanted that and that it could happen, but only once.

Back to our buggy and to explain just a little. The buggy had no tongue or fills attached. They most likely had been removed on purpose, probably when stored. In most cases this could be accomplished without using any tools, similar to todays quick connect attachments. A tongue is used when using a team of horses. The fills were used if a single horse was pulling the buggy. Fills are like two small tongues, one on each side of the single horse.

The importance of the tongue on a wagon I already knew. I had grown up with the men using a team of horses on the farm. No tractors yet. It didn't take a big boy to drive a tired gentle team. The boy could drive when the adult was loading hay or picking rock or many other uncomplicated, safe jobs. There were some jobs a little too dangerous or complicated for a boy to do and with some of them, like skidding logs, we were not even allowed very close to where they were working. The year before my father purchased a tractor, I had graduated to doing the plowing with the team on a level field with a sulky plow, one that you rode on. Tiring yes, but what an ego trip!

Back to our buggy again. The importance of a tongue or fills was considerable as that is what steered the wagon. The steering of one of the

Ed Jr. plowing

old-style wagons was not always easy on the equipment or on the horses. Because the front axle pivoted in the center, when one of the front wheels would come up against a rock or drop in a hole, the tongue would be pulled sometimes quit violently toward or away from that side depending on whether it was a hole or bump. When dropping in a hole the wheel would be pushed forward, then when it came to rising up out of the hole it would be held sharply back, creating a whipping action of the tongue.

We were, when we started to plan for coasting down the sloping meadow, not aware of this, at least not to the degree that it actually does affect the force exerted on the tongue. Just a small rope attached to the axle out near each wheel, with one boy holding on to each rope, should hold the axle straight and direct the wagon down the slope, at least in our overly simplistic expectations, thus giving us a good ride. The buggy would have no tongue out in front to dig in the ground, nothing to stop us from getting a wonderful buggy ride.

Now comes the hard part. We could steer it adequately—that is what we thought—but we had to get up to the top of this meadow, or at least up partway the first time. We kind of knew not to try too much the first time, but to try it in shorter, safer runs. Maybe this came from sleigh riding on a new ski-bottomed sled we had built. Best to try only part of the hill first. There wasn't a pond at the foot of this hill to slide right out into if we got going too fast, but crashing into the shed or missing that and getting out into the middle of the highway wouldn't be good either, or if we didn't steer right we'd get stuck in the ditch. Any place would be warmer than that pond. The best would be to just gently stop before exiting the meadow. But we knew just saying "whoa" wouldn't do any good.

We quickly learned we weren't strong enough to just push the buggy up the hill. By cranking on a back wheel we seemed to have more leverage, but this wasn't going to work. Because of the roughness of the ground the front wheels would not keep going straight. The buggy would very quickly be going sidewise on the hill, not up it. We had to direct where the buggy was going all the time. Okay, we would each crank on one of the front wheels. That way we would be directing where the buggy was going while moving it up hill. But trying to spin or crank on the front wheel didn't work very well either. If I cranked on my wheel harder than Howard did, then mine would go forward but his would go backward. The buggy would barely move, if it moved at all. We were working against each other.

One of us on each front wheel wasn't going to work where the ground got steeper. We were about out of time, as Howard was just able to move his side now and when it got a little steeper, he wouldn't be big enough to do it. Okay, if we move one front wheel as far uphill as we can and then block it, we should be able to both of us crank on the other front wheel and make the whole buggy move. Worth a try.

There was an abundance of stone, at least our wheels kept running over them, but we could not find one that would work for blocking the wheel adequately. Maybe the wooden homemade un-used milk stool would work. It wasn't easy to get a wheel to go up over a rock when trying to roll the buggy and yet we were afraid any stone wasn't high enough to keep the wheel in place when that is where we wanted it.

The first time we got to try for a ride wasn't that night. It was time to go to the house, as the men were done milking and supper would be ready. We would come back tomorrow night during milking.

I do not recall much about working at moving the buggy up the hill after we got started. Guess what we did was quite repetitive. I do know we had to get a little farther up in the meadow to get to where the grade was steep enough so the buggy would roll downhill sufficiently to ride on.

We had a system worked out so we could get in the buggy, get a hold of our ropes, then let it coast. There were no brakes on the buggy so we must have used a block that we could pull out from in front of the wheel with a rope while sitting on the buggy. None of this turned out to be important. We were not going to be able to coordinate with each other in order to steer the buggy with our ropes. The whipping action of the front axle was just too forceful. We would only go a very few feet before one front wheel would get stopped and yank the rope away from the one of us on the other side. The front wheels would get pulled to one side and cause us to come to a quick halt. Because we were going slow, the buggy would not tip over, but would just stop. We were quite disappointed that our project did not give us the ride we wanted.

It was a good learning experience, this "boy work" with a buggy, but by just waiting we were going to be able to ride in that buggy most any place with a horse pulling it. This was my father's ultimate plan all along. He purchased a third horse and semi-retired the old horse Ned before the next crop season. It took very little energy to hook old Ned up to the buggy and then to drive

Buggy rides were more fun with Ned

him. Our "boy work" had taught us well and we were better satisfied to travel on leveler ground, or roadways or lanes where we should. With the availability of a buggy with a good set of fills attached and a gentle old horse, we then got in many a good buggy ride. We only had to harness up one old horse, hitch him to the buggy, pick up the lines and say "geddi-up."

Boy Work, Too

1942
A Lesson Well Learned

My cousin Jim, who was very close to my age, was visiting me for the day and what we were going to get involved in was not all that intelligent. I think we both knew it from early on, but we were just a couple of boys who wanted to sleigh ride without spending too much effort while doing it. For some reason we had the ability to prod each other into doing things we ordinarily would not get involved in.

It was wintertime and we were two twelve-year-olds. This was back when roads were often slippery because the town did not salt or sand. The snowplows were not used extensively either, only when the snow was deep. Otherwise, just drive over it. This often left the road with packed snow on it. The center of the road would sometimes be mostly bare of snow because trucks with chains had chewed it up, thus the center would not be good sledding, but along the sides a sled with steel runners would slide very nicely.

Even with good winter snow conditions for sledding the situation along our main road left some problems for us boys to solve. It was just too level along our farm's frontage. Unless we walked a goodly distance to the east, something over a mile, or accepted a small, unacceptable hill to the west, we needed something to propel us along.

Why not pull it with a horse? Good idea. We even had the use of an old army saddle, which was in our wagon house, so we would have something with which the horse could pull our sled. And one of us could ride the horse while the other was on the sled. Wonderful idea! Except Ned, the draft horse we used as a saddle horse was old and was never made to run, even at a slow speed. My father purchased a third horse to replace Ned and then he was just kept around to do some single horse raking during the summer. Having a third horse didn't help us, as Ned was still an old horse that should not be pushed to go faster or work harder.

Why not use Ned's previous teammate? Prince was a lot younger. He was about twelve years old, not well over twenty like Ned was, and a lot faster. He was a long-legged, shiny black gelding that was just a little high-strung. My father had raised him from a colt. In fact, he had used a friend's big, black purebred Percheron stallion to breed a brood mare that came with the farm when he purchased it. This, then, was one of my father's first farming initiatives that he could call his own. Prince was a very nice-looking horse, but he would have been one of my father's favorite animals even if he had been ugly.

How two preteen boys could conclude that they should saddle a horse that had never been saddled before is now beyond me. If we could get him saddled, how did we ever expect to ride him? I am sure we didn't realize how much difficulty we could be getting into. This included the risk of getting hurt. Actually seriously hurt. I am sure we just assumed we could do anything we wanted to, as Prince had been used as a draft horse day in and day out and was very reliable. I don't think we even considered using Judy, the new horse. She was slower and a complete unknown.

Putting Prince's bridle on was easy. I had done that many time before. I then backed him out of the stall and tied him to a post so as to saddle him. I'm sure I wouldn't have tried to saddle him while in his stall, as it always made me nervous going in beside a horse in the stall. I wasn't any taller than the horse. I don't think the top of my head was even as high as the lowest part of the horse's back line. He could squeeze me very easily against the stall wall and he could kick the hell out of me, as I would not be able to get away. If a person went toward the front, and the manger, then, as I was always warned, a horse could bite bad.

Even when saddling him on the driveway we were cautious. Knowing that he was easily shaken and that this was not a normal procedure, we were very slow and cautious when putting the blanket on. Then, when I was trying to put the saddle on, I didn't want to give Prince the idea I was throwing that big object at him. Do it, but do it very cautiously. Done. Wow, done! Reaching under him to get ahold of the cinch web wasn't all that bad. I had to reach under him every time I put his harness on to get at the belly strap. I had a system—I would put my hand on his side and speak to him, then reach for the strap, bring it over and loosely buckle it. I did the same thing and got ahold of the cinch web, brought it over and slid a separate attached leather strap through the ring. The leather strap was then slid through another ring on the side of the saddle where it was drawn tight—real tight—then knotted with itself. It was a special knot that would lay flat against the horse or against the blanket and would not come loose. The one big thing about this is, most horses do not like to have the cinch drawn tight, but it is necessary to keep the saddle on. Some horses learn to puff themselves up when the cinch is tightened, so later the saddle will be loose and need to again be tightened. Prince, not ever having had a saddle on him, would not have done this. He could have objected with violence, but did not.

Unbelievable. We had just saddled a horse for the first time and had encountered no problems. I am sure it never entered our minds how extraordinary that was. We were innocently getting ready to have him pull a sled, without a thought of how little a chance we had of accomplishing our goal. To get this nervous horse saddled without incident was very unlikely; now we were just planning on tieing a twenty-foot-long rope on the front of a sled and to a ring in the back of his saddle so one of us could ride on the sled. But that wouldn't be the tricky part. If there was ever anything that fit my father's favorite phrase, "boy work," this was it. What were we thinking!

I was actually in the saddle on a horse that had never been ridden before. How unlikely is that? I had no experience riding a horse that had not been broke to ride. No experience at all with any kind of horse that may not follow the rules. Would he even steer right? He sure would not neck-rein, not that I knew how to do it anyway. Even more unbelievable, we were going up the road with me riding an unbroke horse pulling a sled with my cousin riding on it.

I am not sure why it was decided to turn around where we did. My horse was not responding like I would like. He pranced across the road then stepped off the road in the snow where there was some stone fill. Something seemed to spook him as he turned and jumped sidewise, throwing me on my butt on the ground where the stones were. I got up, but Prince had already moved away from me. I yelled at Jim "get off of the sled."

"Why?"

"Get off of the sled!"

As Prince spun toward the barn, his rump caught the rope, literally snatching the sled from the other side of the road where Jim had been riding on it. The empty sled catapulted across the road, still right side up. Then, because Prince started moving so fast, the sled spun around and almost jumped toward the barn as the rope came tight and yanked it again. As Prince was galloping to the barn, the rope would whip up in the air, then hit him on the rump, causing him to increase his speed as he went. He turned left a little, went into the barn and directly into his stall. About the time he stopped, the sled crashed into the side of the building.

I do not remember the aftermath of the incident, except to know that when I landed on the stone, it started me hurting. My father must have taken the saddle off his favorite horse, put the rope away and set the sled inside until later. I was hurting where I could not see it. My parents determined that a doctor should look at it. Dr. Flint said it should heal by itself, but did put a little sulfa powder, a new drug, on it. I never did see what the injury looked like, nor, even though I was hurting, like for real, did I voice any complaints.

The Smell of Electricity

1937

We were having Neighborhood Club at our house. It was a fun time for all the neighbor kids and I know the adults enjoyed themselves, too. Once a month, except during haying time and maybe Christmas in our farming community, somebody would volunteer to have club at their house and everybody would come bringing a dish to pass. We always had good food.

There would be ten or a dozen families there. On this Saturday a lucky electric fence salesman just happened along. He undoubtedly hadn't had any luck finding farmers home in this neighborhood, not yet, but now something was going on.

It was after dinner on a nice early fall day and my father, out of politeness went out to talk with him. Neither one of them wanted to interrupt anything unnecessarily. "What do you want?"

An electric fence to keep cows in a pasture or wherever you wanted to keep them was a new concept. It was something to look at, but seriously question. Would it work and was it practical?

My father was always willing to try something new, with some discernable discretion, of course, but he liked the possibilities.

The salesman had battery-powered units with him to show or sell and Dad had posts and wire and, best of all, cows near by. Let's set up a little experiment.

Now there was a spot between the machinery shed and the highway that was neither lawn nor meadow, nor pasture, nor bare roadway. It had nice green re-growth or after-feed on it. And it was the size of a baseball infield. This would be ideal for a small fenced-in yard made with an electric fence.

Six or eight wood fence stakes were picked up from in back of the shed, plus a part roll of barbed wire, and a crow bar, a fencing mall, and an ordinary hammer from in the shed. All of the men there were very familiar with the process of fencing and well conditioned for that kind of work. Just one thing negative, most of them were in their Sunday go-to meeting clothes. They would have to be very careful not to get dirty or damage their clothes and handling barbed wire was very tricky.

The salesman explained that a smooth, bare, one-stranded wire would be ideal, but seeing as regular barbed wire was the only thing available, it would work just fine. About the only other wire on the farm was some baling wire that had been saved from when some hay was purchased. It was not in long enough pieces to be used as fencing, but it would work as ties to wrap around the wire and the insulator to hold the barbed wire in place.

The salesman must have had insulators with him, as no farmer would at that time possess such a thing. A fencing insulator was a porcelain knob with a hole through it that accommodated a nail which could be driven into the wood post. It looked kind of like a spool that thread comes on except it had extra grooves in which the tie wire was wrapped to secure the fencing wire.

There were insulators used for power line and home wiring needs, but they were big or not well adapted for fencing needs. Later on a "farmer fix" was to cut a small strip of old rubber inner tube, wrap it around the wire and then that was stapled to the post. It worked but when wet it would some times leak electricity to the post.

Many of the earlier fencing units would not work well if there was any kind of leak. Most of the modern day units will work and cause a shock even with a minor short or leak.

Briefly, the electricity that a fencer or electric fencing unit puts out has its voltage and amperage changed and only charges the wire for a brief moment six or eight times a minute. This will cause momentary pain but is not life threatening. With the use of modern pacemakers or other such medical devices there is the possibility of danger.

Many stories are told about people getting unexpectedly tangled up with an electric fence, some humorous, but usually not to the one directly involved.

A few years later my father had a new hired man who was watering the bull. The trough was a shallow cast iron trough. The trough extended out from the fence just a little on the outside and plenty far in on the inside for the bull to drink. The hired man got two pails of water from the milk house and poured it into the trough. Not following a caution warning, he just dumped it in haphazardly and the water slopped up on the bottom electric wire. He instantly threw the pail way out in the middle of the barnyard. At least it wasn't in the bull pen. It was easy to retrieve.

An electric fence wire installed to the inside of the bull pen's wooden pole fence made purchasing a fencer worthwhile. With just a couple of wires attached to the lower poles the repairing of the fence was eliminated. The bull had not torn the fence apart even once since it was electrified.

Soon after Dad had gotten the electric fencer he put up a fence next to the yard by the side of our house. He put his four sheep down there. One Sunday my grandmother was visiting for an afternoon and was out looking at the sheep. She had been told about the electric fence, but unthinking, had taken hold of the post and her thumb touched the wire. Her reaction was normal and they laughed telling her she should listen to her son. The next time she was visiting she told us that the painful arthritis in that thumb had gone away and she could use it like normal.

It couldn't have been the power of positive thinking, it must have been electric fence therapy.

My wife's sister and family were visiting one summer afternoon and her teenage nephew was along. He had his nice fishing pole with him, so he spent some time digging some worms. Putting them in a tin can we gave him, he went whistling down toward the brook. We were using electric fencing in a couple of meadows down that way and had a bare feed wire strung overhead going to the other side of the brook. Georgie, happily walking along, nonchalantly reached up and touched the wire with his worm can. I never saw a tin can thrown any further than that can. Where to find more worms? Bet if he was told not to relieve himself anywhere near an electric fence he would heed the warning.

But, back to the day that the fence salesman visited. All the men from the neighborhood club were there and the fence for a mini pasture in front of the shed was quickly completed and a fencer hooked up to the wire. Spacing of the posts could be at least three times as far as normal as there was no need to have the wire drawn real tight.

By using a long, mature piece of grass one could sense the electrical charge and tell if it was on without getting a jolt that hurt. By holding on one end of the grass stem and touching the other end to the wire, then gradually sliding your hand closer to the wire, it will increasingly provide a better contact. By doing this you will gradually get to feel the shock. Stop when you do. Most of the men had to try this for themselves.

Three or four of the men went across the road to where our cows were being pastured and drove four or five cows up. They were then put in the experimental yard. They immediately went to eating the lush grass. When a cow came in contact with the fence they would jump a little and quickly move away, but none became agitated or afraid as some of the men expected. It took a very short time for them to respect the one loose wire that kept them in.

The experiment was a big success as far as the salesman was concerned. I never knew if he sold any fencers that day, but we owned one the next year and Dad purchased some secondhand copper telephone wire that worked wonderful for our temporary fencing. This fencing was mainly used along the highway. It did a good job of keeping the cows in, except for once in a while.

We soon got a fencer that just plugged into a regular outlet in the barn and didn't use batteries. It was quite easy to forget to plug it in after closing the gate, but it didn't seem to matter. Cows just respected the wire. Until one young "Ada the Ayrshire" type came along and would always be out if the fencer was off. She must have just touched it and taken the shock, then backed off if the fencer was on.

My brother decided after observing her that she did not take the shock but smelled it. She would come up to the fence real close, wrinkle up her

Getting ready to test the fence, PHOTO BY GWEN DEYSENROTH

nose like some cows did when smelling, then move away if it was on. She did not get shocked at all. Somehow you must be able to smell electricity if you have sensitive-enough smelling.

Very soon we realized what was going on. She didn't need a piece of grass to detect the current. All we had to do was clip the long whisker-like hairs off the top of her nose to keep her in.

Fishing Party

1939–1944

Take an axe, a pitchfork, a feedbag full of oyster shells, and three boys and what do you have?

A fishing party.

Now to be specific, the feedbag isn't full of oyster shells. Only a gallon or so is needed. It would be too heavy and too costly to take a bag full. Howard and I would go into the chicken house and shovel the shells into the feedbag.

My dad fed the oyster shells to the chickens to provide calcium in their diet, thus providing a stronger egg shell that wouldn't crack so easily.

The oyster shells could be purchased at any feed store and were widely used in the 1930s. The shells were cracked up into quarter-inch irregular shaped flakes and bought in a 50-pound paper sack. They no longer use oyster shells as a supplement to feed the chickens.

The fishing party consisted of my brother and me, plus a neighbor boy or two. We would get together after it had been below freezing temperatures for a week or more. Our good friend Bob from across the river was almost always there when the main river channel had frozen over adequately, allowing him to cross over. The Delaware River where we fished was a border for the farm on the north side. So it was a quarter-mile or more hike to get there.

The ice needed to be two inches thick or better to be safe enough to walk on. Most likely during the Christmas season would be the first time we could go fishing.

A few winters the temperature wasn't cold enough, long enough for good fishing very many times. That was quite disappointing for us boys.

Good ice would form on the binnekill first, a section of water where there was little or no current as it was not part of the river proper. No water movement let it freeze quicker and almost always smoother. This binnekill ran for a quarter mile adjacent to the river on our side of the river. The upper end was not attached to the river except at flood stage, when the water would leave the river proper and flood over land to enter the binnekill. Most of the time the water backed up into the binnekill from where it attached to the river. There it was thirty feet wide but narrowed to twenty feet for most of its length. It was only about two feet deep were it entered the river and was less than that on up. Because it was quite shallow with no current, it was safe for ten- or twelve-year-old boys to fish on.

The river itself, after running adjacent to the binnekill, with its swift current actually made a hook cutting south across the end of the binnekill, then turned sharp west again almost in line with the binnekill. The suckers seemed to like the still water of the binnekill so that made for good fishing.

Before we had available motorized vehicles, and it being impractical to hook up a horse, we would walk in the deep snow, carrying with us what we needed. Single file we trekked to the river with the person who had the longest legs going first.

Once we got there ice depth had to be determined. We always took a chance knowing it might

Ed's mother, Letha, Howard and Ed
near the mouth of the binnekill

not be deep enough. By hitting the ice with the axe you could guess at how thick it was. Occasionally we would find that we couldn't go fishing.

One time we found conditions downstream a bit interesting where a section of ice over a calmer water pool sounded hollow when striking it with the axe. We quickly realized that the four inch thick ice was not floating on top of the water. It was suspended like a bridge over the fairly large pool.

Our conclusion: The temperature a few days before had gone well below zero with the river at a high water stage. The calmer pool froze first. Then the water level went down leaving the ice resting on rocks on both banks. Needless to say this was not a place to fish.

We lay out the plan knowing where the ice was thin and where it was safe. We would chop holes in the ice ten to fifteen feet from the swift current if the ice permitted. The holes would be six to eight inches wide, and sixteen inches long. They were lined up two or three across the river, always being careful not to create a possible fracture in the ice.

The deeper the water under the hole, the better the fishing, up to a point. The suckers would not go into the swift water, but circle back scooting upstream.

Making sure the hole was clear of debris enhanced your chances of catching the fish.

We were fishing for suckers, a bottom feeding fish similar to a catfish. The suckers were only good eating in the wintertime. A mud sucker couldn't be eaten anytime. We did see some pickerel, which is a predatory fish and must have been able to stay active in the cold water moving much faster than the suckers. They were also a protected species, so don't let the game warden catch you with one.

A plan was formed with a driver upstream making noise, moving the suckers downriver to where the fishing holes were cut.

The driver would walk quietly upstream carrying his trusty pitch fork and then start scraping the fork tines on the ice. He would work back and forth across the river making the scraping sound, which would drive the fish downstream. There was a technique employed that required the driver to occasionally make some louder sounds and then back to the quieter sounds, trying to not scare the fish but just move them downstream.

He could move downstream quite rapidly at first, but the closer he came to the hookers, the more he would slow down and move sideways. Once he saw the hookers starting to pull fish out of the water, he would go into a holding pattern and try to move the fish under the holes as slowly as possible. Some of the fish would swing back so making sounds continued.

Hooking the fish was a technique in itself. The long handled hook usually had two barbed prongs opposite each other on the same plane. Positioning yourself over the hole on your knees so that you cast a shadow enabled you to see the fish. You became one with the river and could see anything that was in the water.

Waiting for the fish to come past your hole, waiting for the right time, catching the fish on a barb, and pulling straight up through the hole took practice. Because the small fish would come first, the hookers would have to discipline themselves to wait very quietly for the larger fish. Very seldom would we hook a fish that was less than eight inches long.

Hookers had to stay alert with hook in the water. Fish would circle back and another chance to snag them ensued.

Several drives were made, changing off drivers. Occasionally new holes were made to enhance the chance of hooking supper.

With our catch, if we had any, we would head home, carrying them in the feed bag.

Now, what happened to the oyster shells? No, we weren't feeding the fish. They were used in the cut holes that had mud under them. The fish would stir up the mud making it impossible to see the fish. So oyster shells were dropped in the hole, giving the hookers a white background, enabling the fisherman to see the fish.

Before World War II, six to ten farmers would get together and go ice fishing. With really cold weather the river would freeze throughout, except maybe a few thin spots. Two, maybe three men would drive the fish down the width of the main river with the remainder hooking from their holes.

Howard and I were the amateurs, so didn't often go with the men, but one time I remember we tagged along. I watched the neighbor boys in

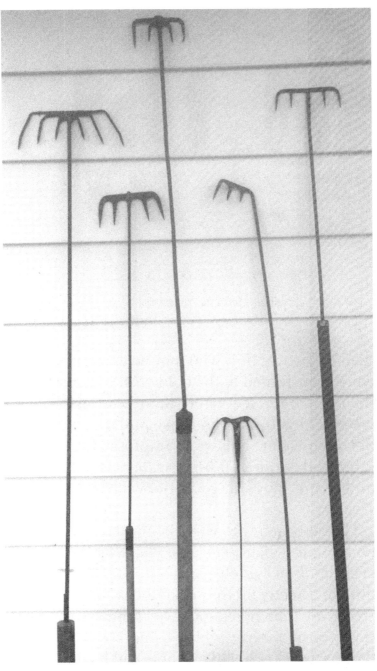

Sucker hooks,
the single-sided and three-pronged hooks were custom made

Sorting suckers, January 1939, Bob Wyer photograph,
Courtesy of the Delaware County Historical Association

their early twenties, who hunted and trapped and were accustomed to the cold weather, walk up to the edge of the ice where there was fast flowing water and with skill and ease pull a sucker out of the open water. This quite impressed me.

Several wore hip-high waders so if the ice broke, and they did go in the water, they would stay dry.

The nine men who were fishing that day brought home almost eighty suckers. There was no effort to keep track of which fish you caught. Fish were thrown directly off the sucker hook towards a safe area away from holes and away from open water, a skill learned early while using a sucker hook. Pulling a sucker out of one hole and having it then flop right back into the river was disappointing.

There was a need to divide up the catch fairly, as not only did the drivers deserve their share but when hooking there was no way of keeping a good tally. When the suckers are running one has very little time, so hook as many as possible. Invariably just as you got a sucker on your hook you would see a much bigger one floating toward you. Get your hook back down in the water quick. No time to check what you just got except to make sure you didn't lose it back in the river.

Eight piles were sorted for the nine men. The reason for that: when one of the last drives was over my brother had borrowed a hook and got down in a hole near to the rocky river edge and was watching. Suddenly he let out a yell and pulled out the biggest sucker I have ever seen. My father said if I get that sucker that Howard caught and one more good size sucker, that will be my pile.

Eight piles were sorted out on the barn floor. The largest fish went first, one to each of the eight piles and then the next largest fish down to the smallest. Once sorted, one of the men would point to a pile, while my father with his back turned would call out a name. This continued till all the piles had been assigned.

This way everyone got an equal share of the fish. When bagged and taken home, the fish made a welcome meal or two or more.

Howard's fish was twenty-two inches long and when cleaned had a six-inch-long sucker in its gut. Maybe that is why we never caught a small fish.

Joe & Wally

1930–1949

I really don't know how old I was when we got
Joe, but he most likely would have been acquired
when I was barely toilet trained, maybe even before. My first memories were that he was just
there. My first dog, actually not my dog, he was
the farm dog, but I guess I thought of him as
mine, at least ours.

We kind of grew up together. Joe had lots of energy and youthful playfulness. I was his substitute for a canine playmate. Joe was a short-haired
brown dog with a head that was just a little too
big for his body. We can only guess at what his
parentage was. He kind of set the standard for my
concept of what a dog should look like. That concept gradually corrected itself over the years, but
not completely.

Joe wasn't a real good cow dog, at least there
are no memories of him getting cows, but that
wasn't my interest back then. He was our farm
dog and being a farm dog would at least have

Joe

been asked to learn how to help drive cows. He most likely did, I just don't recall that part of it.

There are many stories of farmers owning a dog that was an exceptionally good cow dog. Dogs that would, when asked, go get the cows from the pasture, bring them into the barnyard with the farmer doing nothing except maybe closing the barnyard gate. Once in a great while a good dog would, when a cow didn't come or couldn't come would let the farmer know by whining and then would lead the farmer to that cow. Farmers would brag about their dog as being the best hired man they ever had.

A neighboring farmer one day came home late afternoon to find his dog guarding the gate to the barnyard with the cows all in it. That morning he had put the cows across the road into their pasture. They had broken the fence along the road and had gotten out. The dog had rounded them all up, got them in the barnyard, and was keeping them in until the farmer got home so he could close the gate.

Dogs almost always took on the task of guarding the farm. They would at least bark when somebody unfamiliar would stop. This let the family know somebody or something strange was there. They would also chase off stray dogs and wild animals. Dogs tend to be possessive of their territory.

Years later my father had a Great Dane named Sue that never showed any signs of possessiveness or had even growled at a person that we knew of. We had at that time a family renting part of our house and the grandmother was the only one home that afternoon. A man stopped by the milk house next to the road and wanted to get a little water to put in the radiator on his truck that had gotten hot. Sue would not let him out of the milk house with the pail of water. He could come out without the pail no problem. Grandma came out, got the pail, handed it to him and everything was then okay.

Keeping the woodchuck population under control was another responsibility of a farm dog. I do not remember Joe hunting woodchucks, but do remember him eating dead woodchucks on our lawn. The dog that Dad got to replace Joe when he died did have the instincts and inclination to hunt woodchucks or anything that invaded her territory. Wally was part German shepherd and part Collie and she for some reason had an inherited killer instinct. Even flying over head was not acceptable. She would chase barn swallows by the hour. They would aggravate her by dive bombing at her, then swooping away just in time. I have seen barn swallows tempt destiny by swooping down at a cat. The cat on occasion would make a leap to catch them, but I never saw it happen. I have, although, seen a bunch of barn swallow feathers on our back lawn.

While Wally was alive our woodchuck population was almost nil. She would sneak up on a chuck and sometimes beat it to its hole, catching it, and would immediately crush its head if she could get hold of it right. She would break bones, rib cages or whatever with an almost menacing attitude. Many a time she would trap a chuck in a stone wall and would bark and bark until somebody came to help her get the chuck out. Sometimes the stones were too big for us to move and

Wally, Ed, and Howard

the hunt would fail. Sometimes we could use a stick to poke the chuck until it came out and Wally could get hold of it.

One time she had cut a chuck off from reaching its hole by the brook and it had climbed up a small tree. Wally was barking up a storm and when we went to see what Wally wanted it was quickly evident she had treed something. She was looking up and jumping up against the tree. She so much wanted to climb the tree. Nobody had ever seen a woodchuck up a tree before.

When she was young and we were playing or teasing her sometimes she would let us know she wanted to quit. She would nip us, not enough to hurt, but yet it did. One day she nipped my brother a little extra hard and made him mad. He grabbed her tail in both hands and bit her tail so hard she howled. A truce was immediately called.

Wally had one disgusting trait with her catches. She would take them off and bury them. I expect this was instinct, to hide her food supply and keep it for herself, but they weren't refrigerated and when she decided to retrieve them they were ripe and smelled to high heaven. Now, seeing a dog eating a fresh kill was bad enough, but it would turn your stomach when the carcass was half rotten. If I don't want a dog licking me, especially my face, and this includes any dog, anytime, I hope you can understand.

Wally's killer instinct was good in one way, but had a big downside to it also.

One day she was running around our concrete swimming pool, barking her head off. When we went down to see what was going on there was a skunk that had gotten into the empty pool and was not able to get out. Wally could not let that skunk invade her territory. She wanted that skunk out of there and dead to boot. She had tangled with at least one skunk when she was younger and knew quite well what would happen We kind of scolded her, called her away from the pool and placed a board that would work as a ramp for the skunk to climb out. Wally must have positioned herself at a distance to guard the ramp, but did no more barking. She was still determined the skunk had to go. Later that day when she came within 25 feet of anybody they knew instantly what had happened. No matter what the consequence, that skunk had invaded her territory and would not be allowed to live. With that smell so repulsive to a human, can you imagine what it must be like for an animal with an even keener sense of smell?

There was one other incident that happened at least twice with Wally.

We had started growing chickens and selling them ready to lay. They would be started inside and put out into range shelters as soon as we could. This was one more thing running around on Wally's turf. Cows were fine, horses okay and she would tolerate cats, but now all these chickens that were just seasonal were a bit much. There were about a thousand chickens to a batch. We found half a dozen dead chickens at the end of the first day that we put them out on range. She was severely disciplined the first time and again the next year when we caught her in the act. Along about the third year we were ready and preempted her from killing any chickens. Wally quickly, after the first day, became accepting of the chickens and would run along beside the jeep right in the midst of the chickens as we scattered the grain for them to eat.

We had another dog living here for a while that belonged to a family friend. Jenny rented the apartment in our house. This was when Inky, the matriarch of our cat population, was still in charge. She was the undisputed boss of almost everything: cats, dogs, mice, and even rabbits. I think she bossed us humans as well, if we would just admit it. She was an excellent hunter and provider for her kittens. One day she came into the backyard dragging a half-grown rabbit to feed her kittens. Her dominance may have been the reason Wally tolerated cats.

When Jenny moved in she brought with her a small, brown collie-type dog. She was afraid for our cats as there were none where she lived and Jenny was sure the dog chased them off or killed them. She didn't want to tie her dog up unless she had to. When they first got here, her dog bolted out of the car, having seen the cat through the window. Brownie lowered her head and came charging directly toward Inky, who was on our back steps with her kittens. Inky instantly charged at her adversary, jumping almost vertically up in the air just as Brownie got there and landed on the new dog's back. Everything was happening so fast it was hard to know just what was happening, but the dog disappeared around behind the house with the cat on her back swatting at the dog's face. The dog was yelping in pain and moving even faster than when she was charging at the cat. The yelping stopped on the other side of the house and all was quiet. Inky came strutting calmly back around the house, went over and lay down on the steps again. After a few minutes the dog made it cautiously the rest of the way around the front of the house, went up to Jenny and would not leave her side until they were in the house. The next day the dog could not see out of one eye and only see out of a slit in the other eye. Her nose was swollen so that I'm sure she must have been breathing through her

Howard, Edward, and Joe

mouth. I don't think Brownie intentionally even got close to a cat, any cat, after that.

When I was young and Joe was young he was a better ball player than I was. He was always there with us and when we didn't catch a ball he would have it and we couldn't get it away from him for love or money. I was pretty good at teasing my little brother, but Joe was even better at teasing us when he got the ball. He would lay it on the ground near us, move away, then beat us to it every time. We would get so mad at him and I have no doubt he enjoyed it. I could throw the ball at him to hit him just as hard as I could and he would catch it, even when it was a bad throw.

George VanKleek, a family friend and neighboring farmer, years later talked about stopping in during milking when our whole family plus Joe were in the barn. When he came in, I was mauling the dog and being really rough with him. Apparently, I was somewhat irritated with Joe at the time. George said something to my father about how rough I was. Dad said he didn't get too bothered about it anymore as we were pretty evenly matched, and besides, the dog could run faster than I could if he wanted. I was about three years old. Before George left, Joe had me by the collar of my barn coat and was yanking and dragging me flat on my back, down the barn floor. When I tried to roll over, Joe would yank me sideways and flip me back on my back.

I can't remember that. Guess it is a good thing we don't remember everything.

Things to Smile About

Charley Thorington, our neighbor to the west, had sold off his cows in order to have the hernia operation that the doctor said he needed. This operation was considered to be advisable, but back then it incapacitated you for quite a while. They kept you flat in bed for two weeks, and then you were given mobile privileges slowly after that. The idea was changing about then as they realized that being immobile wasn't necessary, and could be detrimental.

Soon thereafter WWII started and the army did experiments with the GIs and found that walking the next day was actually helpful for a speedy recovery. Normal physical activity quickly followed. Guess the stitches would hold you together.

Charley decided that farming wasn't all that it was cracked up to be. Maybe selling insurance would suit him better. My father never had much use for insurance salesmen. He said that they would travel in packs of at least two in order to outtalk and power persuade you so as to sell you something you most likely didn't need, or had enough of, or couldn't afford.

Charley didn't seem to get going on his selling very fast. One day I heard my father tell another neighbor that Charley was "enjoying poor health."

My Dad also laughed about a girl who stayed home from school one day because she had "a touch of the measles."

* * *

My great-aunt Lida, my grandfather Byron Nichols' sister, would almost always visit us each year during the summer. Everybody enjoyed their visits as she and Uncle Jim were always full of fun, down to earth and easy to talk to. Mom always said she liked having Aunt Lida visit. She would write and tell Mom the exact day and time when they planned on getting here and what day and when they would leave. There was no guessing about meal planning.

One year, Lida had a hernia operation that did not hold or stay. They did it a second time and Jim said they went down to the local hardware store and got their very best copper screening and used that to help hold the tear closed. We knew better, but it was fun anyway.

The adults often took their ease on the home-made lawn furniture under the old Northern Spy apple tree during the day and evenings. We kids would play in the sandbox and do something nearby, kind of listening when it interested us.

One day there was a clap of thunder and Jim jumped up. "We better get Lida in the house; she could attract lightning like a magnet." Again we knew better.

My grandmother, Sara Roberts, was a poor speller and I take after her. I sympathize with her completely. Her two sisters were both teachers and good spellers. Sara and Ella were at a church social where of all things, they had a version of a spelling bee.

My great-aunt Ella became quite frustrated with her sister Sara for goofing up so much and like a typical sister finally asked her why she didn't keep her mouth shut and not show her ignorance.

Sara's reply, "What's the matter, Ella, you know Webster and I often don't agree."

* * *

Dad told about a local strict old Presbyterian pastor that like many in small villages kept chickens for their own egg supply. Most churches provided the pastor with a manse, a barn to keep his horses and wagon in, and sometimes other small buildings. With progress, the horse barn would become a garage for a car. This pastor had chickens in a small yard beside the chicken house near a driveway that went down past a store to the church shed. The church shed was a building where teams of horses with carriages hooked on were kept while the families were attending church. I suspect they were used during the week when somebody had occasion to want shelter for their horses while doing business in town.

As chickens will eat almost anything, the pastor's wife would throw all her table scraps and cooking discards into the chicken yard. This was standard practice, so when she had some cherries that went rancid she just tossed them out with the potato peels. The next thing the pastor knew there were people standing looking at his chicken house. Upon checking, he realized that his chickens were falling down drunk. At least they were staggering like drunken men. They couldn't walk a straight line and many could not even get up to walk at all. The cherries were not just rancid, they were well fermented.

It took quite a while before the good natured comments abated about a strict teetotaler becoming associated with, or maybe even promoting, a questionable lifestyle like this. After what must have seemed ages to the pastor, comments and humorous notices subsided.

Wonder if the pastor and family were short of eggs for breakfast for a while. A cow that gets too many apples will become inebriated and dry up or quit milking until calving again. A cow, because of her digestive system, can make her own alcohol; a chicken must ingest it, but maybe they too quit producing. Wonder how the pastor's wife felt about purchasing eggs at the store next door.

* * *

My mother just seemed to have a green thumb. She grew a big productive garden for years. When my youngest brother Denny was about six, Mom, with just a little free time on her hands, got into growing and breeding African violets. She would cross pollinate different colors and then grow them to see what colors or combinations of colors she would get. With only one south-facing window in the kitchen and only one in the dining room, good space for her plants was limited. My father had added onto the window sills and made an upper shelf to accommodate more trial plants, but things were still crowded. One day Denny came into the kitchen and after looking the situation over commented, "Mom, you are just going to have to rent window space from the neighbors."

* * *

There were creameries all over our area, located all along the small railroad line in our region. In previous decades farmers could only get their milk to a creamery by horse and wagon. It had to be taken every day, which was a time consuming chore each and every morning. When reliable trucks became available to transport the milk, distance was no longer so important. Farmers then had several choices. With several companies owning different creameries along the railroad, plus one co-op owned creamery, there were many choices for farmers.

A good neighbor from up the side road had been going to the nearest creamery for years but had been convinced that he would get a little more for his milk at the co-op. He had done the paperwork needed and signed his new contract with the League to ship milk to them.

Now instead of going west two miles to Bloomville like he had done for years, he would now have to come down the mile and a half on his dead-end road and turn the other way to go the three miles east to the League creamery in South Kortright.

There was a good view of the corner from our kitchen window where my father ate breakfast. The first day Dad commented, "first of the month, Frankie is now taking his milk to the League. He will have to change PO addresses, and buy his groceries at a different store."

The second day Frankie came buzzing down the side road and turned toward Bloomville. He went about a hundred feet and stopped, then quickly backed up to the corner. He then went the other way to South Kortright.

"I guess Frankie is going to need a little help with this." Dad got two posts and a wide pine board plus some red paint. Setting up the sign in our meadow directly across from the side road he painted "League Creamery" with red arrows pointing toward South Kortright.

It worked; that was all the help Frankie needed.

LEAGUE CREAMERY

* * *

My father had agreed to having the county "field day" at our farm. Clarence Denton was the county agriculture agent, the man with the necktie who was in charge. His agency had grown, so now he had a full time assistant named Whiteman.

It was 1953 and the planning had begun back in the winter for a hay harvesting demonstration day in June. It would be only ensilage that was actually harvested as the weather was far too iffy to try for dry hay. Machinery dealers from all over would have tractors and all kinds of harvesting equipment there on display.

They expected from a hundred to two hundred people there and needed to make plans. One field had to be cleared or have the hay cut for car parking. One field would be needed for an equipment display area and one more close-by field with a nice crop of hay still uncut would be used for harvesting demonstrations.

Rent-a-johns or spiffy-biffys hadn't been heard of yet, at least not in our rural county. They were sure there would be need of those types of facilities. To some people they would be very important. After some discussion it was decided an unused bull pen would become the men's room.

Denton and Whiteman, using materials Dad provided, put together a temporary outhouse behind the horse barn for the ladies room.

The field day went off very well with few problems occurring. Our farming went back to normal very quickly with nobody showing up for incidental things that would disrupt our routine work.

A few days later as three of us were coming out of the barn a car went swiftly by.

My eleven-year-old brother recognized the county car and waved. "There go the outhouse boys."

Jess Dibble's Pigs

Dad worked for Jess Dibble, a next door neighbor to the Lamb farm, where he learned things not taught in college. He always laughed about teaching pigs to jump. Jess had gotten a couple of just-weaned pigs in the middle of the winter, so he wanted to keep them in the cow stable where it was warm. He got a couple of two-by-sixes and fashioned a narrow pen against the wall in front of the cows. It wasn't too long before the pigs could get over the twelve-inch-high wall so he added another two-by-six. Again it wasn't too long before the pigs were climbing over the eighteen-inch-high pen. Again he added another two-by-six that made it twenty-four inches and then again, thirty inches, which was as high as most pens for big pigs. But thirty inches wasn't going to be high enough for well-trained jumping pigs like these when they got big.

Jumping Horse

One of Jess Dibble's teams of horses would run away. When Dad went to work there he was told to be careful. He should have taken the warning more seriously. They did run away one day when Dad had just gotten done spreading the manure. The manure was spread by hand with a dun-fork and that fork, when not in use, was carried behind a metal tie rod across the very back of the wagon box. The rod held the two sides of the box together. The easiest way of putting the fork behind the rod was to bend over the back of the wagon just a bit and slide the tines in the space behind the rod. Just as Ed went to do this one morning, the one horse jumped forward, jerking the wagon forward, thus dumping Ed on the ground. He had to walk back to the barn carrying the fork. Under normal circumstances, most horses, when running away, will go back to the barn where they are kept. If the wagon is not damaged by hitting something along the way, then no harm, no foul. Ed opted to keep on using this team, but he had a plan. Every time he went to put the fork away he kept his balance well toward the front of the wagon. He was always ready. It was a good thing, because after a while the horse tried it again, but this time when the horse jumped ahead, Ed stayed in the wagon. He took the fork back up front and applied it's tines to the closest end of the erring horse. After making a couple of trips around the big field in high gear he drove them back to the barn. Ed was always ready after that but did not need to be. Lesson learned, for both man and horse.

Mules

To most people the word mule does not have a very positive connotation. To my father it was quite the opposite, as he liked working with mules. I am not sure when mules were first kept on the farm but Theron St John liked mules and kept at least one team of them when he was operating the farm. My father having spent much of his growing up time on the farm with his uncle had had lots of time to get acquainted with these animals and decided for himself his likes and dislikes.

First we will check out a mule's negative aspects. Number one was their potential for being stubborn. They were notorious for this trait as evidenced by the saying "stubborn as a mule" which leads to a story about my uncle "Gid" (Gideon Lesley Nichols).

Gid was living with his aunt and uncle, the St. Johns, and working on the farm while still in school. He was the one who was taking the milk to the creamery every morning using a team of mules to draw the wagon. It was winter time and cold. One day the one mule that had a history of stubborn episodes decided to just stand in place part way to the creamery. Physical punishment or encouragement were not productive, as usual. Gid walked back to the nearest farm where he borrowed a piece of heavy rope and a spare horse. He secured the wayward mule with the rope to a close-by tree. He then separated the mules and, by pulling the wagon tongue side-wise, got his borrowed horse hooked up with his remaining mule and was off to the creamery. He did not stop for the mule on the way home but left him there overnight in the middle of the winter. The next morning he gave back the borrowed horse and rope, hooked his repentant balky mule back to his milk wagon and delivered his milk with no signs of any problems. The mule was not known to cause any problems after that.

Mules are supposed to be stronger than a horse of the same size and smarter. To me the last seems questionable. Dad always said they would not spook like a horse. They kept their cool. A horse would kick wildly if startled, but a mule would only kick you as planned. They would hit their target. To me this did not seem to be a big plus.

Dad would talk about hunting woodchucks with a mule. All he had was a .22 rifle, which has a short range and not much killing power. It is necessary to get quite close and have a chance at a very accurate shot, Because woodchucks were accustomed to cows, horses, and mules and felt

Either my father, Edward Lamb Nichols, Sr. or my grandfather
W. Byron H. Nichols plowing with mules

no threat from them, Dad would ride his favorite
mule while hunting and could thus get quite
close without spooking the chuck. By sliding off
the mule on the opposite side from the chuck, he
could lay the rifle over the mule's back and get a
good shot. The mule would stop with a very soft
command from Dad and hold very still, not moving even when the rifle was fired.

The legs of a mule are a little smaller than a
horse's legs and they usually have a thinner face,
but the biggest noticeable difference is the ears. The
ears of a mule are quite large, taking after their sire,
a donkey, and most mules are smaller than their
brood mare, again taking after their sire a little.

A team of mules taking hay to the old threshing barn, c. 1915

Dad had a saying describing a mule's social position: "No pride of ancestry and no hope of posterity." Mules cannot reproduce. The only way to get a mule is to breed a jack or donkey to an equine mare. What mules you see, if you do see any, are generally the size of a race horse, not a draft horse. The most noticeable exception I've seen were mules owned by the Amish. One farm had two teams that were almost the size of Belgian horses. They must have used a Belgian or Clydesdale as brood mares and had a very large jack as the sire.

A mule has a different stomach system than a horse and is smart when it comes to eating. If a horse gets out from its stall and gets into the grain, it would eat too much. This would cause the colic or overloading of its system and one would often hear a farmer saying that they had to

Ed Nichols, Sr. (front), Theron St. John
and Uncle Gideon Lesley

walk off the colic in a sick horse. They would literally take the horse where they could walk the
horse and keep the horse moving, however long
it took. They would know the horse was better
because the horse would stop kicking or stomping and acting like it was in pain. Mules apparently don't have this problem; in the first place,
they just know when to quit eating.

The mule is a ruminant; it has three different
stomachs like a donkey. A horse only has one.
Why the mating between a horse and donkey
would even produce an offspring is a mystery to
me. This must have been one of the original hy-
brids. Because they are ruminants, mules can utilize fiber like hay better and need less to eat to
live. Even within a species some animals, for no
apparent reason, will take less fodder to maintain
a good weight.

I, when in my early teens, went to a dentist, a tall skinny man who often would tease me about my weight. "You eat too much." My response to him, "No, I'm just a easy keeper."

An easy keeper: A term often used when selling or praising a mule or horse.

A female mule in the early 2000s did reproduce.

Mules typically cost more to purchase than a horse, likely because they don't reproduce.

Mules are hardier and tougher than horses under adverse conditions.

Mae West

World War II was in full swing and I was just eleven years old. I knew almost nothing about war or fighting of any kind except with my little brother. I knew it was not a good thing, both fighting the war and fighting with my little brother. It was kind of frightening, actually very frightening, at times. I did not read the paper, but I had got in the habit of listening to the news on the radio. I was learning names of places that I had never heard of and some I could hardly even pronounce, at least not correctly.

The country was in trouble, real trouble. All the news from the Pacific theater was bad. It seemed like the Japenese were pounding the stuffing out of us, we were losing one island after another. Would they just land in California and march east? Men were being killed, sometimes many, many of them and some were being taken captive.

At that time I had no knowledge of exactly how bad it was to be a captive of the Japanese. We later, in some cases quite a lot later, found out some details, like the Bataan Death March. One of the young men from just across the river had been captured and later said that they had cut the end off of his tongue.

Two other young men who grew up as next door neighbors to us were at Pearl Harbor's Hickam Field on December 7, 1941. The older of the two brothers actually made a valiant effort to tow planes from the flight line where they were easy targets. They both survived the war.

After the war, a man who had worked for my father on our farm before the war was doing some contract refrigeration work in our milk house. He had survived the latter part of the war in the Pacific theater carrying a gun. Something happened, not sure what, a movement, a noise, a smell, whatever, that reminded him of his service experiences. Stopping in his tracks he looked the situation over briefly and said. "If I ever get myself into a real tight place, I want an Aussie protecting my ass." When asked, the only explanation he offered was, "They are the best; they will stay with you till the end." I am sure the incident in our milk house bore no resemblance to the "tight" places he had experienced; it was just a reminder of where he had been.

Another just-returned veteran, while helping his brother on the farm, was driving the tractor, loading hay. When there was a pop or snap from a stick or something breaking, he was almost instantly on the ground, tight to the wheel, having turned the key off on the way. Getting up kind of sheepishly he explained, "that sounded just like a 25," the Japanese standard issue rifle.

The country's troubles weren't just to the west of us. They were east of us, too; they were across the Atlantic in Europe. It seemed like the Germans were going to bomb our ally, the British, right off the face of the earth. Whole cities were just devastated. You took any positive thing that was reported and just hoped that it was true and that the bad things reported were overblown, knowing fairly well they were not.

Many of our neighbors, family, friends and relatives were actively engaged in the fight for what seemed to me to be our very survival.

There was a neighbor boy just out of school who was in Britain flying for the RAF. He had, after getting a pilot license here in the USA, gone over to England before we entered the war and joined the RAF as a pilot. After we were in the war for real, things of all kinds were kept secret, so they most likely would not have known where he was. All the Americans who were flying for the RAF could, after war was declared, transfer to the USAF.

There was also a gal, a next door neighbor, who got a pilot's license while attending secretarial school. After flying transport for the Air Force early on, she transferred to training Air Force pilots as a civilian instructor.

The Germans were in control of most of Europe, moving toward Russia, and were well established in Africa. Early on, the British and Americans were doing alright in North Africa, but that was not much to hang your hat on.

In the Atlantic our ships were being sunk. U-boats were off our coast causing us to practice civilian defense drills. Lights out, civilians patrolling roads and standing at intersections according to a government plan, plus airplane watches everywhere. As it turned out about the only thing that accomplished was to create insecurity. Thank heaven they were never needed. During the last part of the war, when we were winning, the insecurity went away.

As an eleven-year-old and then twelve, as the first year of the war dragged on, I ended up taking on many farm duties to help my father, who was running a farm without enough help. As a 13- and 14-year-old I increasingly took on the work of a man. I do not ever remember feeling that I was put upon or asked to do too much.

There were so many others whose lives were in constant danger or who had inconceivably hard jobs to do. Feeling sorry for myself never occurred to me. Some of what I did I most likely would have been doing even without a war going on. I loved being with the men doing important and interesting work. So much better than sitting in school doing unimportant things.

Many of the boys my age that I knew were involved in working for some labor-short business or farmer. This included before and after school as well as vacations. Family vacations had pretty much been scratched. Few were enjoying the usual activities of young teenagers that would have been their lot if there had been no war. The possible danger that our nation and its people were in was real to me and what I did was well worth it.

The government had set up a program called farm cadets that signed up teen boys from the cities. They lived and worked on a farm for the summer. Our next door neighbor had one such guy. He was nice and apparently quite smart, but it must have been a challenge for our neighbor to orient him sufficiently to make him really useful.

By the end of the summer I'm sure he could do a lot more things and bet what he had learned was beneficial the rest of his life.

One morning after chores, my father, brother and myself had gone up to the neighbor's for a reason I do not remember, but we three boys were working on a machine of some kind, adjusting or repairing. We had taken some of our small tools with us. It was quickly apparent that Rick had had no experience with tools at all. He needed to acquire rudimentary knowledge and skills that up until this time I had just assumed a boy was born with.

For two of the four summers that the war lasted we had help with haying. Things were a-changing. One of the men did not get board or room with us as was usual for farm help. He was picked up about eight in the morning and was taken home, a distance of about five miles one way, just before chore time at night. He did things other than haying, but was hired by the week and was here only one month. Farmers had to compete with wartime factory workers' wages.

I would many times get to do things that I had never done before, but had watched done many times, like putting the harness on the horses. When I first started to do this as part of my chores I was so short and the horses so tall that I could not lock the buckle on the collar, which was at the top of the horse's neck. I would climb on the manger planks or stand on something. The harnesses we used were the britchen type and were a little heavier and a little clumsier to get on than some. I would literally have to throw the harness up on the horse. The horses were harnessed while in their stalls, which meant there was no possibility of getting a running start. The hames were buckled into the collar on the bottom side so that was no problem and the belly strap was gotten hold of by reaching under the horse and pulling it over to buckle it. Except for their bridles, the horses were ready to be hooked together, but weren't hooked up until first thing after breakfast when the stables were cleaned.

I had chores to do before breakfast and chores to do after breakfast before going to school. Before breakfast the chores were generally feeding the calves and heifers, harnessing the horses, feeding the bull, pushing the hay up to the cows and then cleaning the manger. After breakfast the cow's tails were untied and then they were let outdoors. Now, for all the wise guys, the cows were not kept in the barn by tying their tails; the tails were tied up off the floor to keep them clean. The stanchions are what held the cows in.

Next my job was to get the ensilage fed, which took some time. The ensilage was thrown out of the silo into a pile the day before and the cart loaded up with the first load. A cart load would feed about 6 or 8 cows, depending on how much Dad wanted to feed that time of year. If one hurried, this could be completed before it was time to go to the house and get ready for school.

A tub bath was out of the question timewise, so it was a complete change of clothes and a good washing of the hands, arms, and face. There must have been a tell-tale scent left behind me as it wasn't too long before I and one other farm boy were given an early period when a senior boy would get us once a week, take us to the shower room and instruct us to take showers. It didn't bother me or Bob either, we had a good time and we always took all the time allotted. Can't be it worked, as shower trips soon stopped.

The smell of silage is a strong smell that permeated everything and would migrate from clothes to skin and then back to new clothes. It would take a complete change of clothes, with them never getting near each other and a long hot bath with some smelly stuff sprayed on to boot. Poor city slickers, they would have to get accustomed to the smell. It would be their contribution to the war effort.

One day near the end of March when we got off of the school bus, we saw the team hooked to the wagon with the utility box full of the old milk cans that we gathered sap in. Dad met us and said that the sap had been running good that day and he wanted us to gather sap. We would have to get right with it, as it could get dark before we got back. We did, it was, and it did. My younger brother and I went right up on the hill to the sap bush and did get a lot of sap.

Gathering sap was not a real hard job, but did take a lot of time and a lot of walking. It could be difficult in deep snow. We made it back before it was too dark, parked the wagon next to the sap arch and unhooked the team. Got them put away and had some supper. We got our chores caught up and boiled sap quite late that night.

We had quite a makeshift system, but it seemed to work just fine. Sugar was rationed so the maple syrup and maple sugar would help us meet our needs. I learned to use maple syrup on my cereal and still do a lot. Cans to store the maple syrup in were very scarce. Our doctor offered us big brown jugs that medicine came in so my dad used those two-and-a-half gallon glass jugs as storage for our maple syrup. Getting them properly sealed was questionable. We had several of them full that year. We sold a little and gave some away, but used a lot ourselves. Mom did a lot of canning and needed a lot of sugar for that process.

Mom's system for getting most of her groceries was different back then. She would call the store and order what she wanted. The milk truck driver in his daily routine would stop at the post office and the grocery store. He would pick up the mail and our groceries on his return trip with the empty milk cans. Because of this routine we took our food rationing books up to the store and left them. Milt, the shopkeeper, would then take out whatever stamps were due him after each purchase. Because we butchered our own meat, most of the red stamps for meat would not be used. Milt used the surplus stamps to help supplement the villagers who often did not have quite enough.

We boys did have some time to bang around like farm boys would do. We took it upon ourselves one day to see if we could find any old rubber tires. Now, we were quite familiar with every foot of our open land, but we set out anyway. The only tires we found were two under some hay back under the low-sloped roof over the cow stable. We spent most of an afternoon and the tires were worth a nickel each.

One other Saturday in the fall of the first war

 year we went collecting milkweed pods. Milkweed down is permanently very buoyant and floats on water. The government would purchase it and gin it to take the seeds out of it. I have no record of what they paid for milkweed pods, but we weren't in it for the money. I do not

Milkweed pods on previous page and milkweed floss here
MILKWEED PHOTOS BY PAUL DEYSENROTH

know how many pounds of milkweed down it takes to make a life jacket. No matter how much, it saved many a young man's life. This was a very clever way of acquiring the flotation part of the raw materials they needed to make their Mae West life jackets.

The Strike

Something long forgotten I am sure, was the labor union's push to get the dairy farmers to join their ranks way back in the 1930s. Think about it. That would not be a very logical fit. What does a labor union have to offer a dairy farmer? They are on opposite sides of the issue or as a farmer might say "the other side of the fence."

A farmer is a small business owner and the boss, not the wage earner. How could a union that represents laborers help the farmer earn a better living? This caused a dispute back then that got real serious and something was going to happen.

Even the farmers who didn't want to strike were not entirely unified in their thoughts. Why wasn't there a consensus of opinion?

There are many things that influence the price of milk. The government was one of the bigger factors. They were the ones that put together the milk marketing order and they thought price support programs could control the price of milk and all the by-products. The farmers were supposed to be involved but actually had little say in developing their own marketing system or setting prices.

Politically there was little incentive to keep the price of milk high for the farmer. There were far fewer farmers voting than there were non-farmers going to the voting booth. For the politician, keeping the cost of all farm commodities low to the consumer made good political sense. It is still that way today. The only downside was if the prices paid were so low that many farmers went out of business, a shortage would occur.

We are not dealing with cabbage or apples. They could be put up on a shelf for a while.

Milk cannot; it is very perishable. It had to be sold within a couple of days of when it was produced. Dairy by-products on the other hand, notably butter, cheese, and powdered milk could be kept on the shelf. A by-product is what milk is made into when they have too much milk for people to drink. It's something that will keep, but the milk that goes into a by-product is worth a lot less money.

Supply and demand makes the biggest difference in how much milk is worth. Was the milk being sold for the top of the line, bottling purposes? Was it ending up on the table for drinking, or was there too much milk and a lot was being sold cheap to be manufactured into the bottom of the line, butter and cheese and many other by-products. Supply and demand is something many didn't understand. It can be a big factor in what a product is worth and closely controlling how much milk is produced in order to control the supply side is almost impossible. If the union could have gotten iron-fisted control and told each farmer how much milk they could send, it may have controlled the price of milk. The farmers who saw this iron-fisted control as a possibility were the most opposed to the strike.

Farmers are an independent lot to begin with, and not having control of how many cows to milk and how to manage their calving schedule was almost unthinkable.

Creamery companies had little discretion in the price paid to the farmer. This was controlled by the "milk marketing order" or governmental regulations. The blend price was set by the order and competition between creameries was quite limited. Creamery pricing of any incentives would be small. With the relatively new farmers co-op now handling milk, reliable competition was assured. Farmers owned this creamery business and were selling their own milk; they paid themselves all they could. Competition would have kept them from paying much less, which they didn't want to do anyway. Farmers would just change and sell to a competitor. If they paid too much they would soon be broke.

To me, just a kid, this whole thing was kind of confusing. Nobody should be able to keep us from sending our milk to the creamery. Why would they want to? Could somebody actually tell the creamery what to pay us? Why didn't people want more milk? My father tried to answer the steady stream of my "why" questions. I am sure he got tired of twenty questions, with most of them being "Why?" Guess I was just in the terrible "why" stage of growing up.

Many of the farmers couldn't seem to agree and there were often heated discussions. There were always a few dairy farmers who seemed to be standing way out on the edge of the load of hay when doing their reasoning about some things. The underpinning for their reasoning was kind of shaky, like their footing on that load of hay.

A few farmers joined the strikers but none were local that we knew of and the others who were trying to dump milk were suspected union guys who were hired for this type of activity.

They would gather on the public road in front of the creamery. They would physically stop the trucks coming in to the creamery with their milk. They would then get up on the truck and dump all the milk in the road. What a waste! It wasn't good if just a small amount was spilled in the milk house. This was enough milk to cause a small flood in some places.

The strikers had also stopped a tanker hauling the milk from the creameries to the city and opened the valves, letting the milk out. There was a picture in the paper but I do not know how many times this happened. How would you stop a big tanker if he didn't want to stop? They had a story about them taking some belting and putting roofing nails up through it and stretching it across the road.

A river of milk, Bob Wyer photograph,
Courtesy of the Delaware County Historical Association

The labor union was seen by many as serving its own self-interest and would not serve that of the dairy farmer. Why wouldn't they help the farmer? Could they help the farmer? Maybe they could, but some men just wanted the money and power. We in our rural community were accustomed to people helping each other, except maybe when they were horse trading. Guess there are always a few greedy ones.

The hired man on a farm would be a logical fit to belong to the union. But with this push to grow, the farm laborers were not the union's organizational target; there was little financial benefit for the union. The hired man's membership would give the union very little likelihood of acquiring power or leverage in a business or

Milk Strike, July 1, 1941, Bob Wyer photograph,
Courtesy of the Delaware County Historical Association

marketplace setting. So for all their preaching about representing the little guy, they really didn't seem to care much about these little guys.

The strike affected us very little as a family.

As it turned out the strikers only targeted our creamery toward the end of their strike and apparently our farmers were ready for them.

That one memorable morning the farmers had been forewarned. As the milk truck picked up their milk, each farmer would get on and ride along with his milk. Each brought along their weapon of choice.

The farmers, normally a good natured bunch, couldn't resist a little horseplay. One farmer, a big Scandinavian, got on with two buckets of rocks.

One had big rocks in it; the other bucket's rocks were not much bigger than gravel. He explained that one was for him and the other was for his next door neighbor, a little guy named Kiff. He would throw the big ones and Kiff could throw the little ones.

I do not know what weapons many brought, but I am sure most were substantial. I remember them talking about some who took pitchforks. A fork was a tool that a dairy farmer was accustomed to and had lots of practice using. I could not imagine trying to get up on a truck with all those fork tines pointed down at me.

My father, as usual, was thinking differently. He decided to take a blowtorch. It was one of the old-fashioned ones that use gasoline as a fuel. It had a hand pump on it to pressurize the tank. It would throw a small stream of gasoline ten to fifteen feet or more. A little stream of gas in their faces would deter them from climbing up on the truck with no physical contact necessary.

But it was all for naught, or for the best.

I guess the authorities had decided that it was time to stop things if they could, before somebody got really hurt. The New York State Police got there early before the first milk truck arrived, just like the strikers did. The police commander, with a bull horn, made the announcement: "Move all your vehicles immediately or I will follow my orders and we will smash the distributors on every car here." The strikers believed him and were gone.

The part about the strike that I remember the best is a few cars going by our farm on a village to village dirt road at a very, very high rate of speed. This I had never seen before. Dad said they must be speeding to get to a strike site. My brother and I were forbidden to go anywhere near the road and we could not cross over to the barns without an adult going with us. This cramped our style and was the only direct effect we as kids suffered from the strike.

This lasted only a couple of days but to us kids, unions could not be good.

Many schemes were hatched over the years to get a better price for milk but none with the potential for violence that this one produced.

If there is too much milk, then why don't we just give some away? But to whom? If there is too much milk to begin with, wouldn't there still be too much milk? Just flat out too much milk to drink.

Schoolhouse Gone

1936

This was kind of scary, what was it going to be like? I had turned six less than two weeks before this day, so now I was a big boy just starting school in the first grade.

The teacher was a new hire, whatever that was. But she was nice, I liked her. She didn't seem to be bossy; she was actually helping me, I guess.

I could take off my own coat, but she did show me where she wanted me to hang it. Miss Winter was new to teaching and I was new to going to school so I should make out okay.

This was an awful big room. Only two other places had big rooms. The barn, which made sense, and the church, which was necessary as sometimes it had a lot of people in it.

I had been in here before and it was still a big room, but, why such a big room?

There were only three of us, plus Miss Winter. The other two kids were both girls and older than me. They had been to school before. They lived on our road three farms up. I was not accustomed to girls, not real girls. There was a kid who lived next door, but she was only three, so that really didn't count.

My brother and I knew she was different. We were sure of it. She would come over sometimes and play with us. We had a sand box and a swing plus a spinning teeter-totter built by our dad. When my brother had to go inside to the bathroom he would start fidgeting around and stand cross-legged. Then he would tell me he had to pee. When Janet would fidget around and stand cross-legged she would announce she had to wee wee. There must be a difference.

We could see the school from our house and it actually sat on land that had been part of our farm. It took me ten minutes to walk there.

My father was also the school commissioner. That may be why there was no longer an outhouse for the school. They had installed a chemical toilet at the end of the hallway. The kids no longer had to go outdoors to go to the bathroom.

The only door into the bathroom was from the classroom. There was no running water for the school. The teacher must have brought a pail of water when she came. I don't remember if there was a wash basin or not, but for sure there was no tub.

It was therefore not a bathroom, so what should I call it? It was a new room with a chemical toilet.

We had to raise our hand and ask if we wanted to leave our desk for anything, so where should I say I wanted to go?

What to call it was not going to be the real problem. The real problem with this bathroom only happened once. It could have been serious. At least to me it was.

It may have been the first day, I don't remember. It probably was.

I went in and locked the door. I sure felt safer being able to lock the door with all those girls around.

It had the same kind of lock that was on our bathroom door at home. You just pushed a little lever sideways.

When I was done I went to leave, but I could not get the door unlocked.

I tried and tried but it would not move. Finally Miss Winter asked me, "Are you okay?" I told her I was, but that I could not get the door unlocked.

I had decided I was stuck.

There was a window, but it was high up and there was no way I could get it open.

It was too big for me to lift if that had even been possible.

Finally, Miss Winter said she would slide a ruler under the door and then I could use that to push extra hard and see if it would unlock. It worked, I was out. It was decided by mutual consent that it wasn't necessary to lock the door when I was in the bathroom.

I do not remember much about the daily routine of school. Some studies I liked and were easy and others were not. We seemed to spend a lot of time on things I didn't care for.

Was it an illusion or a real necessity? Not sure. Maybe it was necessary so that I could get it through my head. Arithmetic I liked and partway through the year, Betty, who was just one year older, was given the same lesson that I had. I was actually working with or against somebody on one subject.

There were maybe a dozen to fifteen desks in the room, but of course we only needed three.

There was a bookcase, small in size with wood framed glass doors. It stood just a little higher than I. That was our library.

The teacher had a regular desk sitting next to the stove. It was a big wood stove that was a little higher than my head.

It had a tin shield set out from the stove all the way around, except on the front. You could make a fire and take the ashes out through the stove door.

With the shield, kids would not be able to touch the stove where it was really hot. This shield helped radiate more heat.

We grew up around hot stoves, as had the girls. Our stoves did not have a shield. For me any stove with a shield will always be a school stove.

How many teachers would be willing to get to school ahead of the students to start a fire, bringing the heat in the room to a comfortable level?

Everybody there early wore coats until it got warm. With only three of us, all our desks could be next to the stove on three sides with the teacher on the fourth.

What if there had been a room full of kids?

Next to the stove could be too warm and far away could be cold. To be banished to the back corner in the middle of the winter would be harsh punishment.

Our recesses were outdoors except on rainy days. No gym trunks and sneakers.

Sneakers? What are they? I was ten before I owned a pair of sneakers. They were canvas topped shoes with rubber soles.

In the winter, we got our heavy duds on and went out and played in the snow. It did seem like there was a lot of snow back then. Maybe I only remember the fun times in a good snowstorm.

Today there is no such thing as a good snow-storm.

We did build snow forts in the deep snow pushed up by the snow plow. We had snowball fights too, but how much of a fight could you get into with just three kids.

Besides, by the time we got our fort built it was time to go back in.

Did Mom send me in a heavy coat and snow suit with proper arctics (boots) just for recess? No way. I walked the half mile to school. Heavy clothes were a necessity.

If there was much snow I went around by the road.

Walking home was going in the right direction but it was the coldest part of my day.

With a prevailing west wind, going home meant walking directly into the wind. Why couldn't I have a windshield?

Many times I would walk backwards, and then turn around just long enough to check for cars and get going right again.

I never did get so I could walk backwards as fast as walking forward. I did practice quite a bit. Doing a little running was sometimes a good option.

Walking home in warm weather was far more enjoyable.

I don't remember much about learning or how things were taught. I do remember the teacher using flash cards.

What she was trying to get through my head escapes me.

I do not remember where the wood pile was. There had to be one and somebody had to furnish the wood. And I do not remember a car parked at school. Guess the teacher must have had a ride with somebody.

This was true of all four years that I went to the district school. I seem to remember something about a bus from one town to the next, making a loop. I am sure the two older girls had a ride as it was too far for them to walk. I seem to remember them walking up from the corner on the main road.

Being the youngest, I didn't have to arrive until later, so how would I know?

When I was in third grade, Helen and Betty started going to another school, but my brother and Janet, the girl next door, started first grade. They got out of school earlier than I did. There were still three in school most of the time, but now I was the oldest.

I got through the fourth grade in this school and then things really changed.

In 1932 the state education department had started a push to form a central school district, incorporating all the schools in the area.

The school was completed in late 1938 and because of state funding incentives, the central school opened in the spring of 1939, in the middle of a school year.

All the teachers were incorporated into the new central school district and given assignments of classes.

It must have been a giant puzzle to get that worked out. The vast majority of the students would have a different teacher for the last part of the year.

Our district school was different. We chose to continue on through the school year where we were. The following fall we would go to the new central school.

I would be in fifth grade then. Our teacher, Miss Winter, would then be assigned to teach kindergarten in the central school.

Ed, with the schoolhouse visible in the distance—until it wasn't

Kindergarten was a new class that had not existed before in any of our schools.

Our district schoolhouse was then no longer needed by the school system. In many cases, as it was with ours, the land for the school house had been given to the district by the local land owner.

When no longer needed the land reverted back to the farm from which it was originally given. Because the land for District Number 9's schoolhouse was originally part of our farm, my father then owned the school house. All the desks, playground equipment and teaching materials became the property of the new central school district and were removed.

The schoolhouse was soon rented by my father to a family as a summer retreat.

Alice McLean, philanthropist and founder of the American Women's Volunteer Services, wanted the schoolhouse for her South Kortright property.

I was now riding on a 21-passenger school bus going past the old school to my new school, twice a day. I paid little attention to my old school. Then one day I realized that stones and dirt lay along the back of the old schoolhouse, with big beams sticking out.

The next day when I came home the school was gone.

The building still sets on what had been the McLean property in South Kortright. The town highway department moved the old school intact. They used a Lynn tractor to go across some fields, as one bridge was too small. I always wished I could have seen them moving the school.

Necessary Train Ride

I was finishing eighth grade and beginning to reap the benefits of age. We were not required to be in school all day when taking our final tests. We only had to be there when the tests were given, not like those little kids in the lower grades. Many of our tests were Regent's tests made up by the New York State Education Department and administered by the school.

Our tests could be scheduled for both the morning and the afternoon, and once in a while neither. But most of them seemed to be scheduled for either morning or afternoon and nothing the other part of the day. This would lead to an almost wasted half-day. Of course it never occurred to me to study. I guess either I knew it or I didn't know it. How was I to know what I should know anyway?

All the young male teachers had been drafted and some of our former female teachers were directly involved in the war in some way. We were being taught in one case by an older local pastor who took on teaching to help out where he could.

One day my cousin Jim and I each had a test scheduled for the afternoon, but none in the morning. We decided to exercise our freedom and not go to the school until afternoon. This meant getting to school without school bus transportation. They only ran buses before school in the morning and to take the kids home after dismissal time in the afternoon.

Now, Jim lived in Bloomville and there were trains that ran a limited schedule that would take you the five miles from Bloomville to South Kortright and beyond if desired. The vast majority of the business on the rail was freight. We had determined that the late morning train did take passengers and the timing would work.

I doubt the ticket cost us any more than a fifty cent piece, as price controls were still in effect at that time. We were winning, but war worries were not over. No matter, we were going to do something just for fun, just because we wanted to.

The train ride was interesting. You got a different view of the valley than we usually got riding in a car or school bus. Going out of the Bloomville station you started down a slight grade, going past the back side of the old Sheffield creamery where America's first commercial pasteurizing plant had been located. The old U & D railroad, now owned by the New York Central, had a second track, or siding, by the creamery, plus the remains of an abandoned turntable or round house where they could turn an engine around to head it back to Kingston.

The former Sheffield Farms Creamery, Bloomville, New York,
PHOTO BY RAY BRIZZI

That wasn't used anymore. The siding was still necessary as other trains needed to pass the car filled with empty cans that was left by the creamery. This car would be unloaded, then loaded with full cans of milk. The cans would be double stacked or triple stacked, depending on creamery output. A lot of ice would be shoveled into the rail car to keep the milk cold on its ride to New York City. The morning "milk train"

would stop at each creamery along the way and pick up the loaded cars.

If you were going in the other direction out of the station, Bloomville is where the railroad leaves the valley of the West Branch of the Delaware River and goes north toward Oneonta, the termination point. We were told that the largest round house in the world was located in Oneonta before WWII.

From behind the creamery, going east toward South Kortright, the tracks followed near the state highway for a mile then moved south toward the river.

Where the tracks were located close to the river I was able to see our farm and river flat from an entirely different viewpoint. Continuing along the north side of the river, the pines that were located on the northeast corner of our farm were across the river and kind of below me. I recognized the familiar landscape. I knew the area well, but not from this vantage point.

Moving out from behind the pines, the train went along a small river flat where the river had moved away from the railroad, then cut sharply north back across the valley and went under the railroad.

The track continued straight along this river flat in an easterly direction until it reached the Hog's Back Bridge. From here on I was traveling through territory that I had not traversed before. We crossed the river twice more as we came to a long stretch of seemingly level tracks.

The train was not going very fast, but still too fast for me to take in all the landscape and special features I was not familiar with. On this part of our journey the railroad was separating from the main road on the north by a goodly distance and moving nearer to the town road on the south side of the valley. The low land of the valley or river flat was starting to get wider here.

I had never hiked on or hunted on this part of our valley, nor had I helped with the haying as I had with the neighbors to the west of our farm. So this scenery was all new to me.

At the valley's widest point the train crossed a small, almost abandoned road. This road ran in a straight line from the town road to the main road. It went between two farms on the south side of the river, but cut a farm in two on the north side. The school bus used this road for several years. There were buildings at the junction of this road and the railroad. This had been another creamery with a railroad siding to accommodate milk shipments to New York City. There were also two creameries located in South Kortright with their own sidings.

As we neared the end of our train ride the valley's bottom land narrowed rapidly. The rails turned south some as we came into South Kortright. We would be wearing out shoe leather very shortly.

As a side note, I was always told that when the railroad was being built one farmer fought the rail line's construction. It cut his beautiful one-hundred-acre flat in two. The rail line traversed the field near the center of the beautiful flat, making it into one forty-acre field on one side of the track and a sixty-acre field on the other. They say that because of his fighting the railroad, he went bankrupt and thus lost his farm.

There were several much smaller fields along the way from Bloomville to South Kortright that were cut into by the railroad, in some cases leaving just wedge-shaped ends or very narrow strips that made part or the entire field a lot less valuable and more difficult to work, sometimes almost impossible to crop.

It was an ongoing chore putting the cows across the railroad if milk cows were pastured on the opposite side of the tracks from the barn. This was done very little. Two gates had to be opened and closed each time to move cows across the tracks.

From the Hogs Back Bridge to South Kortright was the only section where the railroad cut through the bottom or river flat acreage of the farms. There was a very limited amount of this mostly stone-free tillable land in this area.

When the railroad was being constructed, there was a woven wire fence put up on each side of the tracks except for in villages, at bridges, and a few other places. Each field that was cut into had a ramp built for vehicle crossing with gates installed. These sufficed as the cattle crossings as well. Because the railroad was built with minimum grade changes, the rails were often higher, but seldom lower than the grade of the field it went through. They liked the rails to be elevated so the snow would not drift onto the tracks making snow removal more difficult. Not in the section we traveled, but in some places the railroad put in a type of permanent snow fence to help minimize snow drifting onto their tracks.

In spite of all this, the railroad line did add real value to our valley, even though many individual farms were negatively impacted. This rail line gave all the farmers in the area access to the New York City milk market, meeting one more of the area's transportation needs. Almost everybody wanted the railroad to come to their town, but most farmers likely didn't want it to go through their property.

Jim and I hoofed it from the South Kortright station up through town and at the first farm, walked between their buildings and on down a private road. There was a bridge across the river that belonged to the farm. We used that bridge and private road to get to the main road where the school was nearby.

It must be close to two miles from the railroad station in South Kortright to the school going the way Jim and I did. I had already walked two miles to get to the Bloomville station. Putting the numbers together I had walked four miles plus rode on a train for five miles to get to a school that was about six miles from our house. I had exercised my freedom of choice, tried something different and have remembered it for more than seventy years. Guess it was worth it.

Win or Lose, But Show

4H was something that was suggested to me. Yes, I guess it was encouraged. 4H means different things to different people. To my wife it meant learning to sew under the guidance of Madeline Sanford. She advanced in proficiency as she went from six or seven years old on up until senior high school level. Mastering one project after another included learning to cook, putting together demonstrations, and making presentations. 4H had a large list of projects available to youth of all ages.

What it meant for me now was I would own my own pure-bred Jersey calf. As years went by I had chicken-raising projects several times and just once, a vegetable growing project.

I planted one third of an acre of cucumbers to sell on the NYC market. It was a very good learning project. What I learned was: The smallest size cucumbers bring by far the best money, but, man, it takes an awful lot of them to make a bushel. The biggest ones may not bring money enough to hardly cover the trucking. They have to be dusted or the bugs will eat them up. And if they don't pollinate properly they will grow with one big end and one small end. This only shows up after they have reached large pickle size and by then their market value is gone. Only my mother would use them.

But the most important thing I learned was, you guessed it, I didn't want to be a vegetable farmer.

My father had an all-Jersey herd but none of them were registered or purebred (PB), so in order to get what was desirable I had to get an animal from another farmer. There were many Jersey herds in our neck of the woods and some were purebred herds, thus I did have some good choices locally. The 4H calf club held meetings and demonstrations on what to look for when purchasing a calf and how to take care of them, so I was getting oriented. The age of the animal could also give them an advantage or cause a disadvantage depending on what time of year the show was. Of course, my father kind of took the lead on lining things up. He also paid the bills.

Bill Boggs over in Bovina had a good Jersey herd, so we went there one cold late fall day and finally picked out a PB calf from a nice looking cow. It was important to get the right animal, but they are kind of like people, there is no guarantee how they will turn out.

I do not remember any particulars of taking care of the calf. Early on she was penned with calves from our herd and grew in a normal fashion. I am sure I paid better attention to her, but recall no memorable incidents. What bothers me most is I do not remember her name. All our mature cows had names and I could readily identify all of them and this calf being PB would have had a registered name from calfhood.

One of the big things suggested with 4H dairy projects was showing your animals at the county fair. You tried your best to get an animal that was "typeie" or had an admirable body style. She needed to have good legs under her, a straight back line, deep body, and sharp over the shoulders, graceful neck, shapely head, a well attached udder, nicely placed teats, and many other attributes. These were perceived to be necessary for a cow to be able to eat and digest lots of food, give lots of milk and live a long life. Other things your animal needed to win in the show ring were a good temperament and alert demeanor.

Besides training an animal to lead, stand correctly and keep her head up, prep for a show also could include clipping to help define admirable characteristics or hide bad ones, body blankets to condition the coat, complete bath, hooves polished and hair (tail) brushed out. It was much like a teenager getting ready for a prom.

There are many stories about show prep; some may be true. Leaving the horns on or taking them off an animal was optional at that time and with a Jersey sometimes horns would improve their looks, sometimes not. Nice horns needed to both be the same in size, shape, and color, but of course mirror imaged.

With my heifer the horns that were still growing complimented the face, but needed some correction. I sent away and got horn weights that clamped on the horn and would over time pull the horn down. Her horns were naturally curling in front of her head some, but not enough, so I also got a device with a turnbuckle that would pull them together. It worked wonderfully and as a mature cow her horns were naturally small and now curled toward each other like hooks. They didn't come together but each curled around in a partial circle so that her horns could not hook or hurt another cow.

I do not remember showing her before she was a year old, but I'm quite sure I did. They did have age-defined show classes for young heifers. This was the time when age would make a big difference. It's much like sending a child to kindergarten—if their birthday fell just before the deadline they would be the youngest and could be at a disadvantage.

She was trained to lead and stand correctly well before then.

My younger brother also had an animal very near the same age as mine and a friend, Bob, from across the river, also had a 4H animal, but his heifer was a Holstein, not a Jersey. We pooled our efforts to get to the fair, lining up a cattle dealer to transport the animals. Many supplies were needed, so we put them on Ed Beken's (Bob's father), small stake rack truck and headed for the fair about 27 miles away.

Howard and Ed Nichols with Ed's show calves

These supplies also included things that we would need for camping at the fairgrounds as we would stay there day and night for the week. I think our cattle had to be there on Monday morning, at least by noon, and could not leave the fairgrounds until three or four that Saturday afternoon, no matter what time our show classes were scheduled for or how many show classes we had.

They would not give you any prize money or ribbons if you broke the rules. They wanted as many head of cattle there as they could get for the city slickers to see when they attended the fair. You could get there the day before, as I think we did, because Ed Beken had an RFD mail route to run every weekday morning.

We were assigned a stall or a section of wood rail fence to tie our animals up to, one space for each animal, but it was our obligation to provide all the bedding and fodder, plus pails, shovels, forks, ropes and everything else we would need. There was a water faucet nearby and a water vat under it.

We had to take the manure to a pile outside of the tent that housed the cattle and it was then drawn away by a fair employee. The manure pile was made up of far more bedding than anything else. No way did you want your animal to get dirty. There was much trading of favors and co-operation among cattle owners. The competition was left mainly to the show ring.

There was one older man who had a sizable herd of cattle there. He would get up at two or three in the morning and patrol all the cattle tents. He made sure there were no problems with loose animals or tangled ropes and that the bedding was in the proper place to keep the animals clean.

Cattle show people were not the only ones staying at the fair, but other than those showing equines nobody had to attend to their animals much, if at all.

I had in previous years entered a chicken or class of chickens into the 4H competition. They were taken down and placed in their cages then left in the care of the fair personnel. Their feed and care was provided for the week. There were maybe a few commercial displays that required 24-hour supervision—I doubt it—but many of the midway workers stayed in trailers or campers on the fair grounds.

This, I always believed, lead to an incident with our camping. Our tent was an old one with no sewed-in floor and had to be staked down around the perimeter. My brother's cot and my cot were made up like my father had taught us when we had camped up at Selkirk on Lake Ontario.

We used as our first bottom layer on the cot one end of a wool horse blanket, then put on next whatever blankets we wanted with a sheet laying just under us. Horse blankets were at least as big as a blanket for a king size bed. These were all folded over us in reverse order forming an early version of a sleeping bag, something I had not even heard of yet.

Our friend Bob Beken made up his cot as you would make up a single bed. Bob did use an extra folded blanket under him for comfort. One night, a while after we had gone to bed, I woke up hearing him hollering. After retrieving the flashlight, I found Bob was looking out from under the tent where somebody had pulled the stakes out of the ground, lifted the tent up and pulled the top blanket off of Bob's bed.

Bob had apparently woken up enough to hold on to his blanket, but he was not strong enough to keep the thief from getting away with it. Of course there was nobody outside the tent when we did get to look and the blanket was never found. His bed was remade, folding blankets over from bottom to top so he could keep warm. Not sure why they chose his bed. Did they peek in or was it just their lucky night? I do not think they would have had any success with mine as one end of each layer was being laid on.

There is always one in every bunch and cattle showers are no exception. There was a young man named Dave Orton from near Sidney who was showing ten or a dozen head of Holsteins in the open classes. He was a little too old to qualify as a 4H-er but not much. I think he had some cattle entered in a "herd class," which consisted of several animals, requiring a bull along with some different age females.

The bull he had was just a yearling and as quiet and even-tempered an animal as one would ever want. There were times when nothing much was going on, so boredom would set in and it must have been getting the best of him. He led his little bull to the end of the cattle tent where many people were drifting by, looking around and waiting for the evening entertainment to start. He took the halter off of the bull, slapped him on the rump with the strap, starting him to run. With a loud yell of "bull loose," Dave chased the bull through the walkways between display tents until the bull got tired or Dave couldn't yell anymore, one or the other.

Dave then had to put the halter back on and lead him back to his stall. Not sure how many folks were really shook, but it sure did dissipate the boredom. Some city folks are quite fast.

We didn't make out too good showing our animals, but there were a few ribbons. I don't think Bob made out much better. The first calf that I got was the only exception to our mediocre choices. She had grown to be a nice looking animal and as a bagging heifer took first in the 4H show. Because she was nice and I had hoped she could compete in the open class, I had paid the entrance fee and showed her in the open class. Win or lose, I was in the show.

There was one other animal owned by a Jersey breeder that finally, after much judging time, placed first. My heifer came in second. Not bad, but you couldn't convince me that the judge hadn't placed them wrong. Fancy Jersey breeders have to have first place ribbons or they can't sell their animals.

Boredom must have been setting in again. From down at the end of the cattle tent where Orton had his cattle there was some commotion. There were some canvases blocking the view and somebody was standing on a box yelling:

See the best freak show on the fair grounds. Right this way, see the only good freak show around. Only a nickel a look, see the freak of the decade. Get a look at a live animal with her head where her tail should be and her tail where her head should be. An animal that eats and does everything else like a normal animal should, but whose head is in the wrong place.

It was Dave Orton on the box trying to convince people to pay a nickel to see his "freak" animal.

Finally one of the guys involved told us Dave had backed one of his heifers into the stall. When all was done I don't think he kept even one nickel. Boredom busted again.

I only remember showing cattle two places. The Walton Fair was by far the most interesting, but my brother and I did show cattle at the school fair, if showing was the right term. The school we attended put on a school fair for a couple of years. It was kind of a joke, but kind of fun. There were no rides or midway or anything like that, but the best part was no classes that day.

It was a homegrown affair or do it yourself project. It was during WWII, I believe, and must have taken quite a lot of effort by the school staff to pull off, something we really didn't appreciate until years later.

Of all the things I remember about the school fair, it was not our showing our heifers, but that somebody had brought either pigs or sheep and they had erected an electric fence to keep them penned in. One of the older girls must have had experience with electric fences, as she would get one or more girls to hold hands then she would walk by the fence and grab on to it. For those not familiar with electric fences, when there is a line of people holding hands the one touching the fence does not feel the shock, but the one on the end of the line receives the shock. Rosie pulled this stunt several times that day with a couple of humorous outcomes.

My brother and I were encouraged to take our animals to the school fair that day. They would have adequate space for them in the bus garage in case of bad weather. They decided to put them in the garage even on this nice day. I'm sure the garage mechanic had to wash the floor that night before he put the buses back in.

Showing the heifers couldn't have been very important as I do not remember anything about it. Why should I? Our four calves were the only ones there. But I do remember planning and accomplishing the act of getting the animals there and home again.

We had two animals about 18 months old and two that were about 6 or 7 months old. Even the smaller two were mostly trained at that time. We decided on a plan to use a wagon and the John Deere tractor. We had a rubber-tired wagon with a regular manure or utility size box on it. It was no more than three and a half feet wide and about twelve feet long. The sides were about 12 inches high. Dad had extension side boards that would, at most, make the sides thirty inches high.

The side boards were used when we drew sawdust from the saw mill that was used in the ice house.

We took the back end or gate out of the wagon box. I then backed the back wheels into the ditch near the house where the back would be low enough for the heifers to step in. We checked out places near the school where we would have the same situation. There was a spot close to the school, so we practiced loading and unloading the heifers several times by our house. They learned easily and it was no problem at all. The big ones had to kind of double up to turn around. Their heads would hang over on one side and their tails kind of hang over on the other side, but they would turn around quite good. I don't know how we would have gotten them out the first time we tried it if it hadn't worked. Not sure we had a backup plan, but it worked and with just a few practices, it was a sure thing.

Can you imagine the image of a little John Deere farm tractor going up the road with nothing more than a farm wagon with side board extensions behind it, carrying four heifers, two that looked like they could jump out if they wanted and two boys looking like the cat that had just swallowed a canary? What's up? Hope they are not stealing something.

We were quite happy with ourselves.

Give It a Try

1945

A neighbor of ours, Frank Wilson, was talking to my father when I came around the end of the barn. I needed something from Dad, so I went over and joined in.

Frank immediately asked me if I would do the milking and chores for him for three days while he went fishing up north.

Wow! I wasn't ready for that. Something like that hadn't even crossed my mind. I had no objections to doing it, but would I be able to do it properly?

It was right after WWII and I was only like 15 and wasn't accustomed to working for somebody else, except to help out in haying or stone picking, fixing some equipment or helping with a downed cow. With this I would be on my own. Nobody there with experience who knew the animals or the lay of the land or whatever needed to be known.

I knew our operation almost forward and backward, everything except the financial or bookkeeping aspects. In fact, I and my younger brother

Howard could and did manage things so that Dad and Mom and my kid brother Denny could get away for a few days. In addition, I often would be responsible for a night milking when they went someplace and didn't want to get back in time for chores.

Here was a chance at something new, may as well give it a try. My answer to Frank: "Sure, I would be glad to." I was signed up. With quite a bit of orientation and some planning it should be no big problem. My main concern was I didn't know his cows at all, zilch, hadn't even paid any attention to them when seeing them out in the pasture while driving by.

First, some general questions for Frank: How many cows are you milking? Do you put extra cows in the barn that are not milking? What time do you milk and when are you going on your fishing trip? And, very important, when did he want to get together at milking time so I could figure things out?

I had many questions, just slews of them, but most of them needed to be answered when the milking machines, the feed cart, and almost every thing, especially the cows, were right there in plain sight. This could not be done remotely as I knew nothing of his routine or his cows or his equipment or even his barn.

There would be questions about each individual cow. I needed to see the cow while getting the answers. Were there any cows that needed to be attended to continuously while milking or could I just put the milking machine on and come back in five minutes plus or minus and finish her up? Did a cow have any mastitis (infection) in a quarter that needed to be milked out by hand and or treated? Did any or all cows need to be stripped, finished up by hand to be sure they were milked out completely? Very likely most cows would be handled the same, but there was always the exception, so which ones were they and what was different? At that time they did not have cattle chalk or cattle crayon that would mark a cow and stay on for several days. This came later and was very handy for keeping track of short term things for individual cows. This would have been especially good when I was not familiar with this herd of cows. I just hoped I could remember all the things about each cow when I was doing it by myself.

What milking should I come to observe and get oriented?

Frank was leaving Friday morning and if I was there a little before six it would be fine as he started milking at six. He was milking twenty-one with three more running with the milk cows. Two of them could be fresh or have their calves by Friday. He had a fourth one that was going dry, so he could dry her off and stop milking her before he went.

Well, at least I had a little start on knowing something about what was coming up.

Friday morning I got up a little after five, grabbed a bite to eat. I got in our old 1930 something, GMC dual-wheel, ton-and-a-half farm truck and headed up the road about a mile and a half to Frank's. I had lots of time—intentionally—as the old truck had no doors and was real sloppy in all its joints, especially the one in the steering mechanism that made keeping it in the road iffy unless going slow. The speedometer was broken, but most likely 20 miles per hour was max. I didn't mind, as it was late summer before school was scheduled to start up again and it was just a nice temperature with fresh, clean-smelling air. This was not what most would consider a pleasure ride, but I sure didn't mind not walking. It was even better coming home when I was tired.

What was coming up flabbergasted me. Swear I didn't, but, swear I did. When I got there, Marion Wilson, Frank's wife, came out of the house and told me that the men had decided to leave earlier in the morning and Frank had already gone. What! How much did Marion know about the cows or the system? Did Frank leave any instructions? She knew they were pastured down below the barn and not much more. Did that ever put me in a situation, a bad situation! Like riding a bike to the local store, but doing it blindfolded. I knew how to ride a bike and I knew where the local store was, but how could you ever get to your destination blindfolded? I had never even seen these cows close up before. Was I going to be able to determine, first, were they milking or dry, did they even go in the right stanchions, plus many other things. Guess if they all went in the barn and I got them all hooked up, it most likely

The Wilsons' house and barn

wouldn't matter if they were not in their usual places, least not too much, maybe. But first I had to get them to go in the barn.

The cows were pastured in the meadow down toward the river and there was only one gate so that must be the one to open and let them come up into the barn if they would. But there was no fence to keep them from going right on up to the road or onto the lawn or down the road to the neighbors. This was not the barnyard door that they used most of the year. This was the front door, so to speak, and the cows for most of the year would have gone in the other door. I had checked out the gate system and this was the only way they could get in the barn from where they were. They would have to go in and turn in the opposite direction to which they were accustomed if they were to go into their regular stanchions. I hoped they had done this long enough just recently so they would remember.

I had first put a scoop of grain in front of each stanchion that looked like it had been recently used. It did look like there were two spare stanchions, as the manger was not licked clean.

OK, may as well give it a try, open the gate and pray, maybe prayer had some influence on cows. Couldn't hurt.

The cows all went into the barn. They were accustomed to grain in the manger apparently; at least they all headed for a stanchion. Hope it was the one that they were supposed to go in. I locked the stanchions as fast as I could before any changed their mind. I did close the barn door as quick as all cows were in the barn.

Things looked OK, as far as I could tell. Take a deep breath. Next, at least at home, we gave each cow what extra grain they should get, according to how much milk they were giving. From my standpoint, graining them at this time would have to be the right way to do it, at least for the next three days. Possibly there is once in a while a cow that will not give her milk down (release their milk) unless she was eating grain. Then, with some of those, if you didn't put the milker on within a minute or so after giving them extra grain, the cow may let her milk down and start to leak. This was involuntary; they didn't do it on purpose. They just needed a stimulant to release the correct hormone that then triggered the milk release. If Frank had cows that were conditioned to eat while being milked, I would have problems.

I would have no idea how much milk each cow was giving until I had milked them. How was I going to deal with this? Should I just go down through, looking at their udders and make a guess? I knew this was futile. Many times the size of the udder was very deceptive. Guess I better make up my mind and get going if I wanted to be done by any reasonable time. OK, I would give each one another small scoop, then if a cow gave a lot of milk I would go back and give them more after I was done milking. I could wash the milk pails while they were eating. Now, yet one more thing about feeding them grain. I didn't want to run out of grain. There were only three bags, plus a partial bag. I shouldn't use up all the grain he had on hand. I better be careful how much grain I was using and make sure I had enough for the three days, with some left. Right or wrong, this was my grain-feeding plan. Some cows would get too much, some not enough, I knew that, but "so be it."

Next came milking these critters—shouldn't say critters—Frank had a few real nice looking young Jersey cows in this herd. Cows that were typie with good body confirmation and looked milkie. Cows that with a little luck and a good breeding program could be the foundation for a nice Jersey herd. Cows most farmers wouldn't mind owning, unless he was a Holstein man.

One other thing—I didn't see any calves around. Was Frank one of the farmers who didn't

raise his own replacements? He hadn't said anything about feeding calves or checking on young
stock. Either he didn't have any or Marion was in
charge of taking care of them. Frank didn't have
a bull around either. They had a second small
barn. A horse barn, plus, up the other side of the
road that I hadn't ever gone in, to my knowledge.
Now to check on the milking machines. They
better be in the milk house with the pails, milk
strainer, and milk cans. Yes: I even found the
strainer cloth to put in the strainer, to strain the
milk through. Milk pails were in short supply so
maybe he used the milker pails to carry the milk
into the milk house.

I had been eyeballing the cows, trying to figure
out which were which. If I was right, going by
the total number of cows Frank had told me the
other day and the cows in the barn now, even the
cow he had just dried off was still coming in the
barn. He hadn't moved her to another pasture.
Most likely these were all the cows he owned.
Also, there was one other definitely dry cow in
the barn from what he had said, one that had
been dry a little while, yet lacked a few weeks of
calving.

A third one was due within days and as it
looked, was dry, too. She hadn't calved yet. That
was easy to tell, and it was easy to tell the status
of the one that had just freshened. This meant
there were two cows that were going to be big
question marks. Could I find them? Also, should
you ship the milk from the one that had just

calved? How long had it been? It should be like two days. Guess I would just look at her milk to decide, which again would be very iffy.

Bumping a calf. That was something that I knew how to do, but I had almost no experience at predicting what it meant. If I could bump a calf, how far off was she from freshening? Two months was the magic number. You could bump a calf at three months, maybe even before if you were good or circumstances right, but I wasn't interested in just knowing if they were carrying. I wanted to know if they were close enough up to go dry, or in this case, be dry. It was kind of universally agreed that a cow should be given a two-month rest before calving and starting another lactating cycle.

I didn't want to change anything and didn't need to know anything except to find out which two cows out of the possible dozen questionable cows there in the barn were dry.

I started in mentally sorting the cows, eliminating many of them as most likely milking. A few I could not bump a calf in, so they were put in the milking list. There were a very few that I could bump a big calf and they were put in my "could be dry" list. One cow was bumping a really big calf so she was my choice for a definite dry cow. In fact she looked like she may be just starting to bag. That turned out to be an easy decision.

Now if I only knew which cow he had just dried off, things would be settled. It came down to two likely cows. I would just have to milk both cows at the end and see if I could tell. The recently dried-off cow's milk would not be good to ship if I could tell. The one with the little larger udder had a little mastitis so she was my pick as the just-dried-off cow. I shipped the other cow's milk. Right or wrong. There was actually no guarantee I was even close. Without having cared for the cows previously, it was a shot in the dark.

The milkers were a different brand than we used at home, but I found them together from last night's milking. I did not have to assemble them. He must just rinse them out at night like most farmers did. Got the milkers in the barn with an extra milker pail, and a regular twelve-quart milk pail in the barn, didn't need a stool, so now I was ready to milk. Maybe I would need a stool if I had to hand milk any. Maybe Frank had only one regular milk pail because the milk was carried into the milk house in the milker pails.

Now the need to know where the switch was to turn the vacuum pump on became quite important. The pump is what made the milkers work. Found a switch that looked like it could be the one, but I better trace it out. Did the vacuum pump need any oil or regulating before starting? It didn't look like it. It was very much like the one we had and I did trace the wire back to the switch so, here goes, give it a try.

There were a couple of questions that I had after Frank was back. Did I feed more grain or less grain than he did? How close was I? Also, did I get about the same amount of milk or was it much less? It wouldn't go up with somebody strange doing the chores, not in the first few days, especially someone with no instructions.

Later that fall, a month or two after stabling time, Frank had a tragic fire started by an electrical malfunction that burned his barn to the ground. He lost all his equipment and all his cattle. During Christmas vacation some neighbors got together and removed the frozen carcasses and helped with getting a start on cleaning up. I had been sick abed so couldn't go, which greatly disappointed me, but which may have been a good thing.

Bumps Along the Way

1947

It was fall, and almost dark when we were getting on the train. Something new coming up. We were getting on a train in Utica, New York, with our destination, Kansas City. We were due to arrive there in under twenty-four hours, if all went well. We would have to change trains in Chicago tomorrow morning. That would be no problem as it was very close by with plenty of time. No taxi or bus ride for us, just some walking to do.

Our overnight ride was coming up and we were told we could rent a pillow from the conductor for less than fifty cents. Pillows were advised as we were going to sleep in our seats, but as it turned out they would not be the seats we were starting out in.

The four of us got on with our one suitcase each that we stored overhead. We were on our way to the national Future Farmers of America (FFA) convention. Albert Palm, one of our group of four, was the Vocational Agriculture teacher at my school. Another was George Robertson, a local boy, a graduate from our school who was serving a term as a state FFA officer. The fourth was Walter Gladstone, a senior at another school. He was president of his local chapter and involved with our Delaware County–wide FFA organization. Walt was a congenial, likable fellow who I was to become much better acquainted with in the next few days.

Al Palm was an avid card player; thus he had made plans to help us pass the time while riding. Each seat would flip so that you could face forward or backward. We easily found a place where we could flip the forward seat to look backward so now we were facing the other two in our group. Getting one of our biggest, smoothest suitcases on our laps to serve as a table, we were in business.

We hadn't played pinochle very long when the train came to a screeching halt. Maybe not screeching, but it sure wasn't normal. The train was stopped and nobody was getting on or off. Lights were on, everything seemed OK. The train doors were still closed. After a while we were told that the train had hit a car at a crossing and we would be held up until they got things cleaned up. The people would be OK, but it was going to take a while.

When we got started again there wasn't just the clicking of the wheels on the steel rails like normal. There was actually a bumping along as the wheels turned. It got faster as we picked up speed, which never got very fast. We soon found out the wheels on the engine and those on the first three passenger cars had been flattened from skidding. In order to try to stop before hitting the car, the engineer had put the binders on so hard the wheels locked up. No anti-lock brakes on that train. We were riding in the third car, and this could get to be monotonous. We were bumped along, mile after mile. I wasn't sure I could sleep. It was soon announced that we would be asked to change to a different rail car in Buffalo. When we got there they had called out a cleaning crew to get three cars ready. We could see people moving around in other rail cars on a train track, about four over from us. When told, we took our suitcases and moved across the tracks to our new rail home. If I remember correctly I took my pillow with me, it was mine for the night. We left Buffalo after midnight, much later than planned.

Arriving in Chicago the next morning I think we got our pre-planned train to Kansas City, but we had to hurry. We must have been scheduled for a fairly long layover there. Doubt if they held up their train for our train to arrive, but they may have. As it turned out, it would have been better for a couple of old people if the train schedule had been timed a little differently.

Not sure what we did for breakfast, but I couldn't have gone hungry or I would for sure remember it. They had dining cars on the trains so we were OK. We did eat in the dining car—I think twice—as I remember ordering a fish plate and doubt that would have been breakfast. I had assumed it was a filet or patty, but no, it was the real thing and it took me halfway there to get the darn bones and fish separated. Had lots of time; it just took away from card-playing time.

The train would be traveling southwest and going through miles and miles of nothing but prairie. No mountains or hills or babbling brooks. What we wouldn't give to own a hundred acres or more of this level land back home, with no stones or rocks. Our farm was on the western slopes of the Catskill Mountains and our only level, stone-free piece of ground was six acres. It was the river flat and prone to flooding. Because of the flooding, it had some odd shaped small gullies or washouts. The river flat was one of the very few places where I had ever been on a load of hay when it tipped over.

This was one of our card playing parts of the trip. Mr. Palm's favorite game was flinch, so we three boys were learning a new card game. It was late afternoon and we had played about enough cards when the train slowed up and stopped. We could see no factories or grain elevators, nothing except level land, all that level land. Now what? No way were they stopping to let somebody off. Could somebody have been on the tracks again? It was more likely a cow or could it be a buffalo?

It took time for the news to filter down to us. The train had been going directly at the setting sun. The engineer was driving almost totally blind. He only realized something was wrong when an automobile tire went flying by his window. When he got stopped he had an old truck all smashed up on his cow catcher.

It took a while for them to extract the bodies from the old model-T Ford truck. Some of the details were filled in the next day in the paper. It had been a seventy-year-old man and his mother. Nothing was known why they were there at that crossing at that time. We were allowed out of the train to watch after the bodies had been removed. The crew was using bars and hammers to extract the wreckage piece by piece from the cow catcher and move it off the tracks. When all was cleaned up we were on our way again about two hours late.

What is the chance of riding on a train when they have a car/train wreck? What is the chance of having it happen again in less than twenty-four hours? What are the chances of our charter bus breaking down before we could get to our sleeping accommodations?

It was now early evening and we were waiting for a replacement bus. The bus company would have another bus available soon and they would take us to the Oliver farm machinery show room.

Several big farm machinery companies had emptied their showrooms and put in rows of army cots. That was an economical way to house a lot of boys for three nights. Each cot had two blankets and a pillow, except a few of us didn't have pillows the first night after we finally got to the right cot in the right place. We could use both the men's room and the ladies' room, as none of the employees usually assigned to those buildings would be working. It was still a very inadequate amount of toilet facilities and I do not remember about shower facilities, as I just didn't bother. My mother had packed a wash cloth, towel, and soap and I made do with that.

The bus dropped us off at the Oliver showroom and we waited in line to be assigned cots. Finally somebody told us that the New York delegation was not even assigned to that showroom. They eventually found out we were assigned to the Minneapolis–Molina show room that, thank heavens, was not all the way across town. They would get another bus ready soon and transport us to the new location.

Most of us were settled in by twelve or shortly thereafter, very tired, with our alarm clocks set for about five thirty. Walt and I were scheduled to be extras, as were others, for the pageant that New York State was putting on the second day of the event. This was our first involvement and the first dress rehearsal. We needed to be to the arena, Lord knows where, at seven. At least the toilet facility wasn't busy at that early hour. No food was sold at the showroom where we slept or at the arena that early. We had to find something near the arena.

We were told to take a taxi from where we slept to the arena, four to a taxi, with just one paying. It was at least a couple of miles, way too far to walk; it was actually in another state. I think we slept in Kansas and had our meetings in Missouri because of one minor detail. We had to cross over the Missouri River one way in the morning and back again at night. What a problem it must have been to get the rules for taxi licenses and bus routes and schedules worked out to make their operations legal in both states.

Walt and I did not attend all the meetings. We were not involved in the regular business and had no voting rights so skipped out some, when the agenda didn't interest us. There was a rodeo in another big arena that we went to. We got there early and in the basement level of the arena there was a midway like I had never seen before. I couldn't believe it could be this big. I spent very little money there, but did pick up a couple of souvenirs. Just the size of it impressed me. The rodeo was quite enjoyable, something we would never see at home.

The second day of the convention started out with the pageant and ended with a banquet in the main auditorium for about one thousand. There was good entertainment and good food. The interesting part was associating with different boys from all over. At my table there were three or four from Hawaii. Not a dairy or poultry farmer among them, most likely they grew some kind of produce. The vast majority of the FFA members were from working farms, so we could relate very easily. It was too bad that we were just getting acquainted with guys from other places as the convention was drawing to a close. I guess that is often the way.

The trip home was very uneventful compared to the trip going out. We did have a chance to visit the Chicago stockyards. They were something that we knew about as they were in the news once in a while. They were one of the sources for the setting of most beef and pork prices nationally. Most farm news reports would quote previous day's prices from the Chicago exchange. We did not have an opportunity to observe the financial section of their operations.

We did get to see the enormity of the yards and their system for moving animals around as they came in, their value determined, and then were moved to slaughter. We also could watch from an observation platform, where the trailer carts were bringing the pigs into the slaughter house. They then fastened the pig via a dolly onto a twenty-foot-high wheel where they were immediately stuck so as to bleed them out. The wheel moved them up hind feet first where the dolly automatically transferred to a track that let the pig down into the scalding vat. They were mechanically pulled out and some men scraped the bristles off of them. They moved on out of sight where they were drawn. There were other observation platforms for us where they were cut up, and refrigerated ready for shipment.

We got into Utica the next morning where we had some time to spare before getting our ride home. Mr. Palm went his own way and we three boys, Walt, George, and I set out to occupy ourselves for two or three hours.

There was a self-photo booth near the station. It didn't work very well getting three boys in one photo. George got a cigarette, smoked it down part way, let it hang out of his mouth, put on a very believable gangster look, and took a picture that I bet he never showed to anyone at home. We wandered around nearby streets where there were stores and office buildings. There was nothing of distinction and nothing of noticeable size except the Utica Mutual Insurance building. George commented, "We should see if we can get a tour of that building." Darn if he didn't go in the front door and up to the desk. "Do you have tours of this building?" The receptionist was a little taken aback, but nice and offered to ask a superior. A nice man came out telling us that they usually didn't, but it could be arranged.

First, a sort of an interrogation. The three of us were each wearing our (FFA) Future Farmer of America jackets with our names on them. Were we a political organization? Why were we there? And some other logical questions. He became satisfied we were legit and gave us a good half-hour tour around the building.

I am sure we had all been on an elevator before but for me, I don't remember where. That was the part of the tour that I was most interested in. The building was, I expect, a typical office building, maybe larger than most, close to ten stories high, much higher than anything in our small towns. The elevators were what really interested me. Not only the controls in the elevator itself but the

Future Farmers of America jacket

cables and motors in the attic part of the building. How did they work, how big were the motors, and many other questions that this insurance man was not able to answer completely. Somebody had engineered a good plan to make the elevators work smoothly with what looked like good safety backup systems. Right up my alley.

A part of the trip that I do not think I ever discussed very much, even with Walt, was one of our entertainment activities. In the state of Missouri burlesque theaters were legal and there was one near where our convention was held. We decided to take a once-in-a-lifetime opportunity and go to the show. I am glad we went, but I have spent money on entertainment that I enjoyed a lot more. Back at that time it was quite risqué. With all the changes in all types of entertainment that have occurred over the years, what was presented that day was mild, very mild, in comparison, almost laughable. Watching some family shows, or any soap opera on TV today makes what we saw and heard in 1947 seem mild and not very risqué at all.

Walt and I had arrived at the theater a little early. As the theater was filling up it was interesting to see how many there were coming in with FFA jackets on. Complete lack of self respect just being there, don't you think? We weren't the only ones, but as my father said many times relating to other matters, "That is no excuse." One of the side balconies had a group of FFA jackets in it and we recognized them as guys from Long Island having a good time. They had not been on our train coming out. They must have gone the southern route or by bus.

In thinking back, the changes we have seen in every aspect of life are almost unbelievable.

Changes in agriculture lead the list for me. With the advances in mechanization and technology, some aspects of dairy farming are hardly recognizable. They still need a cow, but even that may change. And the farmer may not have heavy calluses on his hands or wear barn boots much. What about the changes in what is acceptable language or the advances in communications? At the moment I can't think of a thing that hasn't changed. Except old men have gray hair or no hair at all.

Walt and I were really going way out of the accepted norms for seventeen-year-olds that day. Today you would think nothing of it. In fact, I doubt there is even a market for that kind of burlesque theater in the present entertainment world.

In retrospect, it is too bad that the problems that occurred while we were traveling out come to mind first, not the pageant, or the banquet, or meeting highlights. Or how out of place we were or insecure we felt in some of the settings we found ourselves. We were truly traveling in unfamiliar territory.

I have almost changed my mind. Instead of calling this story "Bumps Along the Way," it could have been titled "Hicks in a Big City."

The Right Equine

They said pony, but this one, man, I've seen dogs that big. Well, almost, at least that tall. Oh, well, don't look a gift horse in the mouth. Just because he looks like a barrel with croquet posts for legs doesn't mean he is not a good pony to ride as long as you are small, very small, like no more than fifty to sixty pounds.

The trucker had just led the pony off of the truck. It was the prize for winning the contest that the Grange League Federation Inc. had sponsored. With directions from headquarters, each local store participated in this incentive campaign to help promote sales. The only criteria for a farmer to win was to purchase and pay for the most stuff within a given time frame. It was quite a long period of time, most likely at least two months if I remember correctly.

My father was very disappointed with the pony that they were awarding him for spending more on goods at the Bloomville store than anybody else. His youngest son Denny, soon to become a teenager, wanted a horse to ride and this father would like for that to happen. This little Shetland-type pony just wasn't even close to being big enough and it would get worse as Denny grew. Denny had two older brothers, both six feet tall and weighing in at least one hundred fifty pounds. It was reasonable to expect Denny to be close to that big within a few years.

This pony would have fit right in with the miniature horses that have been so popular in some sections of our country. Denny's father was disappointed to say the least, but was ready to resign himself to the fact that there had been no specifications announced or guarantees made.

John Johnson, the GLF farm store manager showed up before the truck left. He had left an assitant in charge at the store as he wanted to see what they had delivered for a pony. He was somewhat upset. John told the driver to load that pony right back on the truck and take it back with him. It was not acceptable. He called headquarters and expressed his disgust. "Our farmers are by and large farmers whose children would like an equine that is substantial enough to fit the circumstances. They don't want a pony to lead in a kiddie parade, neither are they involved with a circus nor are they running a petting zoo."

John soon called my father informing him they would make a change and a new pony would be delivered. Within a month, a cattle truck stopped and they delivered another pony. The picture opposite, taken by V. B. Cantwell of Hobart, shows

Denny Nichols and John Johnson, PHOTO BY V. B. CANTWELL

the replacement pony with Denny mounted and John Johnson holding the lead rope.

As is evident by the picture this replacement pony, although almost tall enough, is already too small. It was full grown when the picture was taken so it would never be big enough to be adequate. It would soon look and be inappropriate for a large person to ride. Denny and my father started to make arrangements to sell the prize pony to a family with a much younger and smaller boy. Denny had in the meantime been going on Saturdays with his cousin Anne Nichols out to West Kill to teach a girl, Janie Pepper, how to ride and show horses. Anne had been in the business of training and showing horses for a long time. They had several horses there and one of them Denny rode often while there. He had grown to like her. Denny bargained for and purchased Blue Tail, a blueish, light gray roan mare so he now had a horse to ride. Several years later when Denny was no longer here, Blue Tail gave birth to a male colt. She was kept on the farm for several years after Denny was gone.

John Johnson's dedicated involvement was appreciated. GLF had people quite knowledgeable in all aspects of the retail farm supply business. It is too bad they didn't have somebody with more savvy to do their horse buying for them.

A New Breed

1956

We had always had Jersey cows. I can remember no other breed of bovine on our farm, at least through the 1940s, unless a neighbor's cows were out and that almost never happened. But in the mid-1950s things were changing, not by design, but due to circumstances not really under my father's control.

The first change that happened was caused by chickens, of all things. My dad had sold some chickens to a so-so farmer and did not get all his money for them. In order to get his due compensation for the chickens he took in trade four almost one-year-old calves, two of which were black and white.

The black and white bovine is just what you would think, black and white. It is also a colloquial term for Holstein, one of the five breeds of cows kept on area dairy farms. The other four breeds around here were generally shades of brown. These were four distinct breeds, originating from four different places worldwide, with different characteristics.

There are more than five dairy breeds but these five seemed to be sufficient to fuel adequate competition between dairy farmers. Friendly discussions was often heard expounding the merits of one breed or another.

At a neighborhood club meeting, which included farmers representing most of the breeds, a debate developed between a Holstein breeder and a Jersey breeder. A little background first: The Holstein cow was the biggest of the breeds and gave the most milk, but their milk was the lowest in butterfat content and solids nonfat. The Jersey cow was the smallest and gave the least milk, but it had the highest butterfat and solids nonfat content of the breeds. Solids nonfat was not tested for or used as a basis for milk payments until many years later.

The Holstein man opened with the statement: "If I could put a quarter on edge in a pail, the poor little Jersey couldn't give enough milk to come to the top of it. You would always be able to see the quarter. Now any Holstein would cover the quarter twice over." The Jersey owner's response: "Maybe, but I would be able to see the quarter right through the Holstein's milk."

Milk was paid for by the hundred pounds, but as the butterfat content went up, they increased the price per hundred pounds. It was an item of debate if the butterfat differential was too high or too low.

Now having a black and white bovine on our farm was going to take a little getting use to. Looking out in the pasture and seeing these different colored animals, which would eventually grow to weigh half again as much as the Jerseys, would be strange to us. No, they weren't strays, they belonged.

How were we going to explain this variation of color to other Jersey farmer friends? Would we now be able to argue the merits of Jerseys as convincingly as before? Maybe turning a profit was just as important as an ideology. Truly a good arguable point.

The two other nondescript calves out of the four were sold, taking a small loss. They had little potential from all visual evidence. The two that my father kept were soon, with good care, maturing into nice animals, especially the somewhat smaller one. She was not a bad looking bovine at all. By the end of that winter they were bred and would calve the following fall a while after stabling time.

Now, to add one more ingredient to the mix or more accurately, one more breed to the dairy. My younger brother, born in 1942, was getting involved with the 4H calf club at this time. Across the river was a farmer, a good friend of my father and our family. George had a well-established purebred Guernsey herd. He was a generous fellow and through the 4H calf club gave my brother a purebred Guernsey calf.

Uh-oh, here goes, we were not supposed to consider the Guernsey as equal to our Jerseys. Now we may have to look the facts straight in the face. These two breeds were the closest alike of any of the breeds. Jersey milk was just a little richer, higher in butterfat content, but the Guernsey milk, because of its slightly yellow butterfat, could use the logo "Golden Guernsey" on all its labels. They were close of a size and somewhat the same in color. The Guernsey red was distinctive, but not always solid. The Jersey color ran from dark brown all the way up through the reds to fawn and sometimes white patches, mostly on the face.

Raising calves was not always cut and dried. There was a certain amount of care and expertise, with some luck, needed to be successful and the Jerseys and Guernseys were sometimes finicky.

The very young calves, after being fed the mothers' first milk, were put on a purchased milk substitute, which was surplus milk made into powdered milk with some additives put in. It was reconstituted with warm water. Whether real milk or the substitute it was weighed or measured out carefully twice a day and fed to the calves. This would total about eight pounds per day.

Calves do not start out as a ruminant with three stomachs, but develop into one gradually at about three months of age and this development requires them acquiring the right bacteria to make their digestive system work. Jerseys and Guernseys were prone to scours or bovine diarrhea. This would sometimes be fatal. This Guernsey calf started right out with problems.

Just after we got the Guernsey calf, the nicer of the black and white heifers lost her calf early or aborted. She had started to bag nicely before she aborted. Unless a cow was for some reason or another a valued animal, she was often sold, especially if she aborted late in her pregnancy.

Dad decided to try something. The black and white cow did seem to have a little milk in her udder, so he put the Guernsey calf with the Holstein cow. The cow accepted the calf, making her a nurse cow. The pail feeding for the calf was quickly eliminated. This was a very iffy situation the first few days.

Three of four days later it seemed to be working, so why change now? The calf was doing OK and the cow, well, who could tell for sure. The mothering instincts of some cows causes them to produce milk when a calf is trying to nurse, and this seemed to be happening. Guess this could be called nature's hormone therapy

Very shortly the calf, when let out of her pen, would make it to the other end of the barn by the cow in no time flat. In four weeks you could readily see the calf was growing. Its stomach would bulge out when done eating so we were sure the calf was getting lots to eat and it had no scours. Our Jersey calves were starting to look kind of puny in comparison.

We were sure that our nurse cow was producing, but how much? We had our cows tested once a month by Lyle Wilson, a milk tester from the Dairy Herd Improvement Association. Their rules: all milking cows in a herd should be tested once a month, but he could enter a cow on his books as a nurse cow. He skipped weighing her milk and taking a sample the first month. This meant we had no idea how much milk the Guernsey calf was getting. We did milk the cow with a milking machine the next time Lyle came at about eight weeks. We had to feed the calf with a pail that day. We would now know how much the calf was getting, but also would be able to weigh and record the pounds of milk and get a sample to test for butterfat content for the permanent records of that cow.

That darn black and white, chicken-traded cow was giving almost twenty pounds of milk a day, even after aborting her calf. The darn Guernsey calf was a bright, alert calf outpacing our Jersey calves in weight and size, hands down, no scales needed.

Talk about a conspiracy of sorts. One that we were willing participants in, yes, actually helped perpetuate. How were we going to explain this?

No matter what, I was still a Jersey farmer.

But before the Guernsey was a year old my brother was diagnosed with a terminal brain tumor and the calf was given back to George.

The two black and white heifers both gave birth as second-calf heifers to female calves sired by our Jersey bull. They were raised and became good additions to our herd. These two shiny all black, crossbred animals surely did not help our Jersey image.

Digging for Water

1951

I was out of school and working with my father on the farm in a limited partnership arrangement. It was primarily a dairy farm, but we had some poultry on the farm also. Land was limited, so we were opting to expand the poultry part and build a henhouse to hold from two to four thousand laying hens. Many decisions were made in putting this together. First was where to locate it. Then, how big do we make it and how do we make it economical to build and efficient to operate. Many of the decisions were made logically, but as is sometimes the case, some were a flip of the coin.

Hurricane Hazel still had enough strong winds when she got to the Catskills to blow down some of the trees in our woods. The timber from those trees would make good structural lumber for parts of the new henhouse. Job one then became getting those trees cut into the saw log lengths. The sizes were critical as the structural pieces we ended up with depended on the log length. Skidding them out of the woods and taking them the two miles to the mill needed to be accomplished also. The lumber, once sawed, had to be trucked home, or more accurately, wagoned home as we moved the logs to the mill and the lumber home with our tractor and a specially built rigging on a rubber-tired wagon. Some of the lumber was loaded on the mill's truck, directly off of the saw, and delivered. It was easier for them and sure helped us out. Lumber that we purchased was delivered by truck.

The next summer, right after haying was done, we started digging the foundation by hand. What a job! My brother Howard was also working on the farm by that time. We had been haying it and had been doing all the farm work that needed doing. But we were not conditioned for ditch digging in the middle of the summer and were not prepared for the digging conditions we encountered.

Why didn't we just hire a backhoe? What is a backhoe? We knew about a steam shovel. It was a large dirt mover that wasn't powered by steam anymore. We also knew that the town highway department had a shovel mounted on a bulldozer-type machine that they used to load their trucks. It wasn't designed to dig ditch. It was big, cumbersome, and slow. The material was picked up going one way, then with the use of cables, the bucket was pulled up over top of the machine and lowered on the other side, where the bucket would be the other side up and the contents could be dumped. That must have been a really dilly to operate.

The next year, after it was too late for any ditch digging, Bob Cowan, a farmer and businessman in Hobart, purchased a machine that was the first actual backhoe we had seen. The dirt was picked up by pulling the bucket toward the machine instead of pushing it away like all other power shovels we had ever seen. It was still a cumbersome piece of equipment compared to the backhoes and excavators of today. The hoe was rigidly mounted to the dozer-type machine and the whole tractor had to be turned sidewise to empty the bucket in a location different from where the dirt had been picked up.

Delaware County is not noted for having an overabundance of top soil, or easy to shovel gravel. We encountered neither. On the east end of the building site where the cattle lane and the upper end of the old barnyard had been, all the top soil had eroded away. Once some loose stone had been removed, we were already down to the hardpan. Now, all hardpan is not equal and you guessed it—this was a combination of compressed clay and gravel that lived up to its name. If there wasn't a sharp point on it, the pick would bounce when it hit the hardpan. Maybe not, but back then we would have sworn to that being the case. You could not just drop the pick in and loosen up the soil. You had to swing the pick good and hard to have it penetrate at all. On the other end of the site it changed completely. It was what we called bonny. Most likely the product of brook flooding or glacial deposits, it was made up of mostly baseball- to soccer-ball-sized stone with very little dirt or gravel in between.

Our goal was to dig deep enough to get below frost level, which was considered four feet below grade. We never made it and were told by those who should know we didn't need to. Setting a foundation on real hard hardpan was all that was needed. Frost won't heave hardpan. Also, many foundations are set on just a good stone base, which was what we already had on the other end. These were two different sets of conditions, but in the end both worked. The cinder block wall of the hen house laid on top of the poured concrete wall stayed firm. The depth of the concrete wall varied from one place to another with the circumstances. The top of the wall was at floor level for the first floor.

The forms were all built in place, board by board and two-by-four by two-by-four. Rough lumber of varying sizes was used with twisted wire loop as the ties to hold the forms together. The sand, gravel and cement were all shoveled by hand into a batch mixer, dumped into a wheelbarrow, wheeled along plank ramps and dumped into the forms. It took more than a week between chores to pour the walls.

We did have a self-propelled cement cart. We had had earlier that year a field day at our farm with all kinds of equipment and tractors on display and demonstrated. The Massey-Ferguson dealer had left a small tractor that they picked up a few months later. We put a platform on the lift arms and carried our cement out in the morning and put the tractor back under the shed at night. This kept it dry if a rain shower happened to come up at night.

Do any of you believe in water witching? I wasn't sure I did, and I had been brainwashed a little, at least enough to consider it a possibility.

We should back up a little and explain water witching. Some people have the ability, by using a small forked branch or stick, to tell where there is a vein of water running underground. They also can locate an underground water pipe or sewer line. Not possible, couldn't happen, had to be a trick. Maybe. Back at that time they didn't have their little electronic devices that would locate a buried telephone wire or tell where the water line to your house hooked on to the main line. They didn't have people running around with their electronic disks, powered by a battery in a backpack, looking for old coins and discarded goodies from olden times. That technology had not been developed yet and using a forked branch to locate water was bordering on witchcraft.

My father had decided that the spring supplying water to our house and dairy operation would most likely be inadequate to also supply our new henhouse. Instead of digging a ditch between the two buildings and adding the henhouse to the barn system, we would try to develop a separate system for just the henhouse. There was no good spring located anywhere near close enough to even consider, so we were left with two other possibilities: A drilled well or a dug well. A drilled well took considerable cash outlay with no guarantee, but it could be located almost any place we desired. A dug well was a different story, but also came with no guarantee. Could we get water in a dug well located somewhere near the new henhouse? From when the farm was first settled until spring water had been piped in, the house on the farm had been supplied with water from a dug well, so we would explore that possibility.

Now we needed to locate a vein of water, hopefully close by, and the only way we knew of doing this was water witching.

We started by asking around and finding out all we could, mostly who could do it. There was a local man who did water witching, so we hired him to come in and check things out. I remember he claimed to be able to tell how deep the water was below the surface. I recall nothing else about what he did or what he suggested. We also knew that my Uncle "Gid" (Gideon Lesley Nichols), did a lot of water witching and even other things with a witch stick, so we had him come and assess the situation.

Gid explained some theory and what could be determined, much of which proved to be right. He and a few other witchers he knew of could not wear a wristwatch. It would quit running after they had worn it a short while. This was before digital watches. He always carried a big, heavy pocket watch that did not become magnetized like others did. Some men who had watch problems would have more than one watch and would rotate them, putting one back in the jewelry box while carrying another one.

Almost nobody believes, when first confronted with the possibility, that water witching works, especially that one could do it for themselves. Gid would get a small, fresh-cut, very green stick for them, show them how to hold it, get them where there was underground water indicated, then he would step up behind them, taking hold of their elbows. Almost always they would feel the stick pull toward the ground. Hard to deny it worked when the stick was pointing forward and you could not hold it there. It would bend, or twist in your hands. I tried it for myself and found that the stick would bend down without anybody touching me, but it proved to be inconsistent, working one day and not on others. The reason was not explained. My father and my daughter could both do it quite effectively.

Uncle Gid carried this even further. He claimed things that proved to be true, but sure seemed farfetched at the time. With the development of new modern electronic devices and techniques, witching now seems more plausible. Of note are the devices that are used to find hidden treasure.

Gid could find a hidden gold ring with his modified witch stick. Also, he could find magnetic north like a compass.

Back to our new henhouse and our desire for a dedicated water supply for it. All witching seemed to point to the same place or vein of water. It came down under what was the end of the old lane, crossed the old barnyard, and then went under the corner of the haymow and across the road. It went right under the end of the unbuilt henhouse. No reason why, if we designed it right, it could not be dug inside the now newly-poured foundation. It would end up in the storage section of our proposed egg room. This was perfect, as eggs should be stored in a cool damp room. It was a good place for it, except this was where we had given up digging deeper in the hardpan the previous summer.

Thank heaven for Bob Cowan. I don't think we would have made it without his track mounted hoe. He stopped to look at the job and decided he could reach over the new concrete foundation wall and dig a hole six or seven feet deep where we wanted it. He could back up and turn to deposit the material outside the foundation wall. He dug it in less than two days, which was good considering he had to get his tracks close to the new wall, yet not hit it with each hoe full, and how hard the digging was. He was able to dig six to seven feet deep and ended up with a reasonably nice-shaped hole close to five feet in diameter. The top two feet would be made into a rectangular pit, approximately three feet by four feet, that could be covered with a wooden platform. The bottom of the pit was made with a round hole over the well shaft. An old cast iron flywheel from a buzz saw was used as a lid for that hole. When done, Bob had gone down at least six feet, which was as far as he could reach. He was still digging in hardpan. It was our turn next. We had some heavy rains so we had to bail the water out of the hole in order to start digging. Water does not penetrate hardpan, as it has a lot of clay in it. Hardpan is not consistent in the depth of the layer or in the consistency of how hard or how much clay is in it. How could we be so lucky as to be digging where the hardpan layer was going to be more than six feet deep? What a pain! In some places it could be only six inches thick, more or less, and maybe not made of material that caused it to be so hard. This hardpan was very tight.

When digging a well it is almost impossible to do it without two people working at it. One is down in the hole pecking the material loose and then shoveling it into a pail or bucket. It was necessary to use a short-handled shovel as we were only digging about a four-foot diameter hole by hand. The second person is up on the ground level pulling the pails of dirt up with a rope and carrying them away to dump.

The first foot of our digging was in the "Real McCoy" hard hardpan. Then it started to gradually change until we were in a nice gravel layer and the digging was a lot easier. There was water starting to seep in from the upper side, the side toward the mountain. That was very encouraging. We had found water. Right in the location and very close to the depth that the witchers said we would. Some gambles pay off.

We still had to dig on down through gravely soil for maybe three feet to create a reservoir and to be sure we were getting all the water that would come in. We now had to line the dirt sides with stone to keep the dirt from falling in. It most likely wasn't necessary to line the hardpan, but we did anyway. We also needed to create a base to pour our concrete on to form the bottom of the pit and a lip for the lid.

We hauled in fieldstone from nearby walls for this purpose. Originally, stone walls were laid with all the stone taken from nearby fields, no size or shape was excluded. We did not take the stones just as we came to them, but were a little selective as to size and shape. They needed to be laid into a wall in a confined area. They were loose laid with no mortar at all. We ended up with an approximately thirty inch diameter center that a man could get down in if necessary.

This well ended up successfully watering three thousand laying hens with a continuous flow trough system, plus plenty of water for use in the egg room.

A Wild Goose Chase

1969

Almost everybody has heard the phrase "wild goose chase." So, what does it really mean? The meaning will most likely vary a little with each one of us, but not too much. One evening after walking home tired, its meaning came into much sharper focus for me.

I'm sure we have all used that phrase when wanting something that seemed elusive or out of reach. Maybe getting a date, or finding a lost item that just wasn't any place you looked. Could be like going shopping for something you should be able to get easily. Most likely a fairly common item, but still you ended up without getting it. The clerk tells you "The last one sold this morning" or "We don't carry them anymore." You didn't find it anyplace in town.

One evening in the fall of the year, my high-school-age son and I were coming up our drive when a large flock of wild Canada geese circled over our house no more than five hundred feet high, making a terrible racket. They were honking and kind of squawking like they were mad or in distress. The noise they made was not deafening, but very loud. It was evident they were trying to land some place.

The usual flock of geese seen that time of year is often very high up and headed in a southerly direction. They will fly over any time of day, or even at night, letting you know they are there by their honking. The flocks will vary in size, some small, some very large, always flying in a V formation.

This flock over our house was not a monster of a flock, but a large flock and not in formation. There were at least fifty, and more likely seventy-five, birds. The larger the number the harder it is to estimate. Eight or ten geese are easy to count but when you get up to fifty or seventy-five the counting is likely not accurate and probably they are undercounted by quite a bit.

The geese went over our house, turned slightly north and disappeared in about a half mile, down behind trees, stone walls, gravel knolls and whatever rural scenery this farming country provided.

This large flock of geese had landed down by, or quite likely on, the river, on what we calculated to be the second farm west of ours. It was land that had not been farmed very intensely in recent years. It had become considerably overgrown from its glory days and was excellent wildlife habitat.

The river flowing by that farm had long before anybody could remember separated and formed

an island. This was the only island that I knew of for many miles around that had tillable land on it. When I was younger, while helping our neighbor finish haying, I had taken our tractor across a shallow place in the river and mowed hay on that island. I had also helped the neighbor draw the hay off of it.

What possessed us that evening I will never be able to explain. We decided to see if we could find those darn geese. We were sure about where they had landed and that it shouldn't be too much of a problem to find them.

Because of articles we had read we set out knowing full well how clever and stealthy geese could be. When we did get there we could make no noise whatsoever and could not let them see any movement. Good luck.

We spent almost two hours, sneaking and peeking as it got darker and darker until we got tired and gradually came to our senses. There was nothing, just nothing, anywhere, zilch.

Their hearing was better than ours. Their vision was better than ours. They could move without making a sound, especially in the water. We were at a disadvantage, a big disadvantage. That disadvantage may also have included intelligence.

We had truly been on, "A Wild Goose Chase."

Not Just a Mound

The need to preserve food into the winter season has always been with us and for Patrick Lamb it was a challenge. Homesteading in a remote location in the late 1700s and early 1800s and having a good reliable food supply was not an easy thing to accomplish. He needed to be able to preserve his root crops to help sustain himself and his future family through the cold bitter winters. Because he was an Irish immigrant, we would anticipate that his primary root crop would be potatoes.

He had acquired in 1787 the rights to a one hundred-eighty-acre tract of land in the Catskill Mountains. He was going to settle there and make this his own. A home where he would live, and this, heaven be praised, was in America. Patrick built a log cabin to start with so he would have shelter. He was to marry Miss Susannah Brown in 1793. She would be moving from Westchester County with him into the Catskills so the log cabin would need to be big enough to accommodate a small family.

The newlyweds would be living on a parcel of land that was then still part of Ulster County.

This farm, along with others in the neighborhood, would be put under other governmental jurisdiction by the state legislature over time. It is now in the township of Stamford and in the county of Delaware.

Patrick Lamb's recently acquired parcel of land, later to become a farm, was bordered on the north by the west branch of the Delaware River and would go, after more lots were added, to approximately the top of the mountain on the south. It is located in a narrow neck of land projecting west from the main body of the town of Stamford. It is situated with the township of Kortright just on the north side of the river and the township of Bovina just up over the mountain. Often when defining its location, this homestead is still placed in the wrong town by those unfamiliar with the circumstances.

While clearing his land for field crops and pasture, plus for his garden, Patrick lived in his newly built log cabin. He did not have a deed to his land as we now know it. This was before the Anti-rent Wars and the land was owned mostly in very large tracts by wealthy owners that had acquired it with favors from those in power. The small land owners, or actually renters, had an ongoing contract with the owner, and paid rent for the right to keep using the land. Taxes were paid to the government besides paying rent to the land barons. It was Edmund Lamb, Patrick and Susannah Lamb's, son who first got a real deed to this land giving him ownership as we now know land ownership.

Patrick's log cabin had no cellar, as most did not, and thus no good place to keep vegetables. To build one he needed a place handy to the log cabin where it would be easy digging and stay dry. Choosing a spot, he built himself a much needed dirt cellar. Patrick Lamb chose well, as the site that he chose did stay dry, except for the normal dampness that occurs in earthen structures.

This dirt cellar is often referred to as the potato cellar. I suspect that is primarily what has been stored in it, thus the name. I know it has been used at least twice during my lifetime to store potatoes. Because of its underground construction and with a tightly closed entryway, the potatoes always kept well and came out in good condition mid-winter, or later.

The challenge to build almost anything back in the 1790s was far greater than today. This was particularly true of a project that included moving earth, like building a root cellar or underground storage. Not only was all the dirt moving done by hand with a round pointed shovel and sometimes a wheelbarrow, but stone had to be pulled or dragged near to where it was needed by a team of horses or oxen.

The availability of rocks was not the problem, there were plenty all over, but to get them dug out from where they were found, was. I suspect that Patrick, if he had cleared some land of trees and rock before building the potato cellar, had set the stone aside that he anticipated would work well to build this dirt cellar.

Dragging rocks to the site then moving them into position without having the ability to push a rock away from you except by using hand held bars would have been tedious, slow, and hard work. They had devised different systems to allow a team to drag large rock, those too big for a man to move otherwise, to the exact location where they would become part of the stone structure. Drag is the key word here, as often the rock it was to rest on would be moved out of place in the process of placing it.

Building walls or columns out of field stone is difficult and time consuming. Patrick not only had to get the rocks and build the vertical walls, but had to get a few rocks large enough in size and shaped right to make a roof or ceiling that would be tight enough to keep the cover dirt out and to hold the weight of that dirt, plus to keep the rain from seeping down through as much as possible. The difficulties would be similar to those encountered when building an arch bridge. It has to be built so that it will hold itself up when weight is put on top of it.

The one north end of the cellar was just laid up stone like the sides, but the south end needed to have some type of entryway that would accommodate a tight door to keep the cold from getting in and freezing. This hallway, more accurately a tunnel, leading into this potato cellar is long enough to accommodate two doors, one door near each end of the entry way. Pat surely had two doors as he didn't have material to make an insulated door and needed the frost protection.

There have been two sets of doors built in my time as the dampness deteriorates the wood and renders them unusable.

One of these sets of doors was built back during the early part of WWII, before insulation board, when a local grocery store owner, Milton Henderson, had purchased potatoes from a farmer and wanted an ideal place to store them until they were needed by his customers. He had an agreement with my father, Edward Nichols, Sr., to use Patrick's potato cellar. He hired a set of doors built and installed. Not sure who he hired, as labor was very scarce. This old dirt cellar was used again many years later by Patrick Lamb's sixth-generation descendent, Gwen Deysenroth and her husband Paul, who built two new doors. They stored potatoes, carrots, and beets in it when they first purchased the property in 1983.

We have never found any records of exactly when Patrick built the potato cellar. We do know that he had moved into his new framed house by 1804. The house had a cellar under it so an extra underground structure would not have been needed. It is expected that Patrick built the potato cellar very soon after he built his cabin, likely before he was married in 1793.

He built other structures, some of the first ones most likely of a temporary nature. Of the three permanent structures that he built that are still standing there is an old English-style threshing barn now extensively restored by Paul and Gwen Deysenroth, and his post and beam house with an 1840-something addition for his son when he got married. The house has been continually lived in to this day. Finally, there is Pat's potato cellar, the first built of the three.

Of the three structures, the old potato cellar is the oldest, but has been used by far the least. The only change to this some two-hundred-thirty-year-old structure is the changing of the doors.

What is yon hump we see in the ground
Down to the west, just up from the brook?
It's surely manmade, "Not Just A Mound."
Excuse us please, so we can go get a good look.

Patrick Lamb's potato cellar in 2022, PHOTO BY RAY BRIZZI

That Old House

Apartment

When I was real young it wasn't an apartment. It was just storage and some of what was there were honest-to-goodness antiques. That part of our family's old house wasn't used for everyday functional living activities any more. It had been lived in for more than a hundred years by my ancestors. The original part of the house was being built when they changed their calendars from the 1700s to the 1800s and it was not built all in one year. The fireplace that they built on the north end and used to cook in and to heat the house, still exists almost exactly as it was. The upper part of the chimney was rebuilt in the mid-1940s so that it could still be used for a kitchen stove in the added-on kitchen.

For me as a young child, that part of our house was just storage except for the back room that somebody had added on. That room had been used for what my father always called the summer kitchen. When I was eight or nine Dad remodeled

The fireplace Patrick Lamb built, Photo by Ray Brizzi

that addition and used it as a garage for his 1929 model A Ford car, the only car we owned until 1939.

In about 1942, a neighbor, John Swantack, got married; the couple were living with his wife, Mary Swegel's folks over in Kortright up past Doonans Corners. It was a good fifteen miles or more drive every morning, over difficult roads to traverse in the winter, especially at five o'clock in the morning. He had to return over the same roads after dark when he got done with the evening chores if he wanted to be with his new wife. It was also too far for him to go home for the noon meal or any meal, so he ate at least his noon meals up on the farm with his brother, sister and his mother who owned the farm.

In order to make things better for John and Mary, and utilize that part of the old house, Dad cleaned out the space and with what help he could hire in the very early forties, made that space, which was mostly one big room, into living quarters, also tearing off the garage / summer kitchen and building a new kitchen addition. Two bedrooms upstairs in the old part of the house became part of the apartment and within a couple of months after John and Mary moved in, part of the front hall was made into a bathroom so it was no longer necessary to share that facility.

My early childhood memories of that old part of the house were few, but do know as preschoolers we and our parents slept out in the old kitchen when it was beastly hot in our low ceilinged bedroom upstairs in the newer part. The newer part really wasn't so new, as it was built only twenty to twenty-five years after the original part.

I am sure we used the old summer kitchen as a summer bedroom. One week after a beastly hot start that then cooled down nicely, we were getting ready for Sunday School and at the last minute of course, my shoes were nowhere to be found. My brother Howard and I actually went barefoot almost all the while during the summer. To my delight my shoes could not be located and by the time Mom finally realized where I had last taken my shoes off it was too late to go to Sunday School. Going barefoot the vast majority of the summer did create at least one positive aspect for me to remember.

John and Mary Swantack purchased a home in a nearby village circa 1950 and moved to it with their three-year-old daughter Kathy. The apartment was then used by a distant relative of our family after she was widowed. She lived there for a few years until her death.

In later years my parents lived in that apartment after retiring from farming while my brother and family lived in the newer part. Mom and Dad had one room downstairs in the newer part that they used as their bedroom.

My niece and her husband, Gwen and Paul Deysenroth, lived in this apartment when first married and then moved into the newer part when they purchased the farm. My brother and his wife, upon selling the farm, built a new house on part of this farm where the old District Number Nine schoolhouse sat.

Two hundred and twenty years after this house was built, I, a great-great-great-grandson of Patrick Lamb, the first to settle and build here, am now living in that same part of the house that he and his family lived in, but with all kinds of modern conveniences. I often get to wondering what life was like for Patrick, his wife Susannah and their four children back when they were living here, in what was their new home.

The author at work in his part of that old house

Ed Nichols was born on his family's farm in 1930, a farm originally settled in the 18th century by his great-great-great-grandfather. Ed operated the home farm until age 40, then formed his own construction company, which he ran for 25 years before retiring. He then sold firewood produced from the wood lot that was part of the family property settled by Patrick Lamb. Ed wrote on and off throughout his life, often poetry for special occasions, but got into writing seriously during the pandemic.

Made in the USA
Middletown, DE
07 September 2024